Performance
Measurement in
Service Businesses

Lin Fitzgerald
Robert Johnston
Stan Brignall
Rhian Silvestro
Christopher Voss

Printed and bound by Black Bear Press Ltd.
King's Hedges Road, Cambridge CB4 2PQ

Contents

Preface

This book aims to help service managers to develop appropriate measures of business performance to support the creation of a sustainable competitive advantage. Our premise is that the measurement of performance is central to its control: if business performance is not measured, how can service managers claim to be controlling it?

The book is aimed at anyone who is either practising or studying management in service organisations and who is concerned to develop effective measurement systems to monitor and control business performance. It focuses primarily on performance measurement in for-profit service organisations operating in competitive environments, although many of the issues raised and approaches described will be equally applicable to those working in the public sector.

Our contention is that there are three different types of service – professional services, service shops and mass services – and that approaches to performance measurement vary between these three. It is argued that service managers should adopt a range of measures to evaluate the performance of their businesses, monitoring the more intangible aspects which contribute to competitive success, as well as the more easily quantifiable financial results. Six dimensions of service business performance are identified; financial and competitive performance, service quality and innovation, flexibility and resource utilisation. In Chapters 2 to 6 ways are suggested in which managers can approach measurement problems and implement appropriate measurement systems in their organisations for each of these six dimensions.

The reader may observe that many of the measures, signals and numbers discussed in the book are not traditional management accounting numbers. We make no apologies for this. For performance measurement and control, organisations require an appropriate mix of financial and non-financial, qualitative and quantitative measures in order to implement, monitor and develop their competitive strategy. These measures will involve radical changes to the content of most traditional management accounting systems. Thus there is an opportunity for management accountants to play a proactive role in the development of management information systems to support competitive strategies for the 1990s and beyond.

We draw on a wide range of case material to illustrate the issues and show how managers in UK service organisations are currently measuring their business performance. Most of the material is based on a two-year empirical research project sponsored by the Chartered Institute of Management Accountants between 1987 and 1989. We take this opportunity to thank the Institute for funding the research and for its continued support and encouragement throughout the duration of the project.

The aim of the research project was to document the state of the art in current UK practice in performance measurement and control in services. The research team was inter-disciplinary, including academics from the fields of management accounting and operations management.

The team, based at Warwick Business School, University of Warwick, comprised Lin Fitzgerald, Lecturer in Management Accounting and Robert Johnston, Senior Lecturer in Operations Management, the joint directors of the project; Rhian Silvestro, Research Fellow, Anthony Steele, Professor of Accounting and Chris Voss, Professor of Operations Management. Stan Brignall, Lecturer in Accounting and Finance, joined the research team to collaborate in the writing of the book; his contribution has been invaluable.

The following service organisations kindly participated in the research: Andersen Consulting, Barclays Bank plc, British Rail Intercity Birmingham, BAA plc, Thorn EMI UK Rental Ltd, Commonwealth Hotels International Co. and Martin Retail Group. We are very much indebted to the managers and staff in each of these organisations who were most generous with the time and resources they put at our disposal. The insights gained and the findings which resulted from the investigation would not have been possible without their co-operation and full support.

The empirical data was collected by means of in-depth interviews with senior and middle managers from both financial and operations management functions, together with a review of in-company reports and documentation. Control information flows were traced within each organisation from strategic business unit level through to regional or head offices.

The companies provided a wealth of data, much of which has been used for illustrative purposes in the exhibits contained in this book. The views expressed here are those of the authors, and not necessarily those of the organisations studied, or those of the Chartered Institute of Management Accountants.

We are grateful to Myron Bileckyj, Stephen Dobson, Andrew Griffiths and Ceinwen Rowlands who carried out some of the interviews and contributed to the initial data analysis in part fulfilment of their MBA degrees from Warwick Business School.

Finally, the research team thank academic colleagues both within and outside Warwick Business School, who have provided valuable feedback and useful ideas with which to develop the conceptual frameworks presented in this book. Special thanks go to Roy Staughton, University of Bath, for his help in the early stages of the project.

Author Profiles

Lin Fitzgerald, BA, ACMA
Lin Fitzgerald currently lectures in management accounting on
undergraduate, postgraduate and executive courses at Warwick
University Business School. She gained considerable industrial
experience and completed her CIMA qualifications while working for
British Telecom. Her research interests and publications are in the areas
of performance measurement and cost information for management
decision making.

Robert Johnston, BSc, MBIM
Robert Johnston has held several line management and senior
management posts in a number of service organisations both in the
public and private sector. He moved into academe in 1980 and is now a
senior lecturer in operations management in the Warwick University
Business School. He is the director of the School's Consortium MBA
Programme. Robert has written extensively on the service sector. He is
the author/co-author of three books on service management and has
contributed many articles to journals and chapters to books.
He is the editor of the International Journal of Service Industry
Management and maintains active links with many organisations through
his research and consultancy activities.

T. J. ('Stan') Brignall, BSc
Stan Brignall spent 10 years in industry as a management accountant and
has been a lecturer in accounting and finance at Warwick University
Business School for 12 years. He has published research in the form of
books or articles on the Steel Industry, Industrial Policy and Shadow
Planning, Inflation Accounting, the Coal Industry and Performance
Measurement in Service Businesses. His current research interests
include Strategic Management Accounting, Performance Measurement
and Management Accounting in Service Organisations.

Rhian Silvestro, BA, MBA
Rhian Silvestro teaches service operations management in Warwick
University Business School. She previously spent three years as a
research fellow on a research project sponsored by CIMA on control
information for service management, and has publications in the field of

quality management and performance measurement in service industries. She was formerly production manager at Mitaka, a Far East translation and typesetting company.

Professor Chris Voss, BSC(Eng), MSc, PhD(London)
Chris Voss is Professor of Operations Management at the London Business School. He was formerly Professor of Manufacturing Strategy at the University of Warwick and worked in production in the steel industry. Professor Voss has researched and taught for many years in the fields of Manufacturing Strategy, Service and Quality Management, Technology Management and Japanese Manufacturing methods. His recent work has included manufacturing strategy, Total Quality Management, the application of service quality in manufacturing, technology implementation and concurrent engineering. His books include: *Just-in-Time Manufacturing, Managing Advanced Manufacturing Technology* and *Operations Management in Service Industries and the Public Sector.* He is Chairman of the UK Operations Management Association, and acts as an advisor to many companies.

1
Control and Performance Measurement

'Choice of appropriate [performance] measures is an art that must be practised in conjunction with the strategic goals of the firm and in close communication with the rapid changes occurring in firms' . . . processes.'

Kaplan R.S., 'Accounting Lag: the obsolescence of cost accounting systems', Harvard Business School, 75th Anniversary Colloquium on Productivity and Technology, 1984

1.1 Introduction

Service industries are an important and growing sector of the UK economy, functioning in an increasingly competitive environment. The focus of competition is changing – in many cases has long since changed – from simply competing on price to competing on a range of other factors such as quality, product and service innovation and flexibility of response to customer needs.

Managers are having to develop strategies to compete in these dynamic environments. These strategies must take into account such factors as the economic climate, the needs of customers, the expectations of shareholders, the requirements of employees and resource implications. This creates a need for information on these factors. The major function of management information systems is to provide information to help management plan, control and make decisions in their organisations, where their key task is defined as being how to devise strategies to gain and retain a competitive advantage.

Our aim in this book is to describe, for three service archetypes, a range of financial and non-financial performance measures which can be used to support the strategy chosen in response to the competitive environment.

Performance measurement is an essential part of any system of feedback control, but the nature of service businesses poses particular problems in this area. In the remainder of this chapter we first outline the nature and importance of the service sector, then make a case for the use of a range of performance measures across six dimensions; next we describe the three service archetypes, and finally link control and performance measurement in the three service types with strategy and the competitive environment.

1.2 The service sector

Service industries are those included in Sections 6 to 9 of the Standard Industry Classification (SIC). They treat people or provide goods or facilities for them[1]. The service sector is diverse, embracing such things as tourism, financial services, health care, catering and communications.

In 1989 services accounted for 64 per cent of UK gross domestic product (CSO 1989) and this proportion is growing. Since the mid-1970s services have grown at twice the rate of the rest of the UK economy, and this expansion has been mirrored elsewhere in the developed world. Some services such as tourism increasingly support the UK's declining visible balance of payments. In an interdependent economy the growth of the service sector underpins the health of the rest of the economy by providing a competent workforce to manufacturing industry and a demand for its products. 'It is an inescapable fact that services are a critical cost dimension to the nation's manufacturing competitiveness'[2].

Control and performance measurement have been more extensively investigated in manufacturing than in services, but there are four key differences between them which make it difficult to transfer precepts from one to the other. These qualities are *intangibility, heterogeneity, simultaneity* and *perishability*.

First, most services, unlike manufacturing outputs, are *intangible*. They may be performances rather than objects[3].When travelling by air one is influenced by many intangible factors, such as the helpfulness of the cabin crew, as well as more tangible and hence measurable aspects of the package: the arrival of your luggage with you. Customers are therefore buying a complex bundle of tangible goods and intangible services: this makes the service process difficult to control as it is hard to know what the customer values in the process.

Second, because service outputs are *heterogeneous* the standard of performance may vary, especially where there is a high labour content. It is hard to ensure consistent quality from the same employee from day to day, and harder still to get comparability between employees, yet this will crucially affect what the customer receives.

Third, the production and consumption of many services are *simultaneous*, for example, having a haircut or taking a rail trip. Most services therefore cannot be counted, measured, inspected, tested or verified in advance of sale for subsequent delivery to the customer.

Fourth, services are perishable; that is, they cannot be stored. *Perishability* thus removes the inventory buffer frequently used by manufacturing organisations to cope with fluctuations in demand. Therefore scheduling operations and controlling quality are key management problems in services, which are made more difficult by the presence of the customer in the service process. Although the simultaneity of production and consumption enables cross-selling and the collection of feedback from customers in real time, an unfavourable impression of the service process may erode a customer's satisfaction with the service product: which of us has not fumed at slow, thoughtless service in an otherwise excellent restaurant, or despaired at the time spent queueing at a supermarket checkout?

Taken together, these four characteristics pose a unique set of problems for service managers. They will also affect the process of performance measurement, not so much in terms of *what* is measured, but *how* it is measured.

Performance measurement is a key factor in ensuring the successful implementation of a company's strategy [4]. Business and business unit performance needs to be measured in relation to the objectives identified in the planning process. Service businesses are now competing on non-price factors such as quality, innovation and flexibility, which has forced a change in emphasis from internal performance measures like efficiency to external, market-based measures such as customer satisfaction with quality. Recognising this change, academics like *Day* and *Wensley* [5] have advocated the balanced use of two ways of searching for a sustainable competitive advantage, customer-focused and competitor-based, while noting that in practice most companies lean towards one or the other. A company's range of performance measures therefore should include both types of measures.

The well-known study of US companies by *Peters* and *Waterman* [6] identified superior profit performance in companies which aimed to do something well. Many successful firms institutionalise their chosen strategy ' . . . by creating a corporate culture – a set of shared values, norms and beliefs – that has as one of its elements an obsession with some facet of their performance in the marketplace. McDonalds has an obsessive concern for quality control, IBM for customer service, and 3M for innovation'[7]. Whilst such companies have ambitious strategic financial objectives, these objectives are imprecise and always discussed in the context of other things that the company wants to do well. In this way profit is a by-product of doing something well, not an end in itself. This implies that an over-emphasis on measuring short-term profitability is likely to be dysfunctional.

Both the *Peters* and *Waterman* study and a critical examination of traditional management accounting suggest that to be successful firms need a range of performance measures, both financial and non-financial, related to their particular competitive environment and their chosen strategy for dealing with it. Recognising that many firms have reacted to the problems of size, complexity and diversity by decentralising some decision-making powers, this study focuses on control information and performance measurement at the Strategic Business Unit (SBU) level, rather than at the corporate or functional levels.

1.3 The need for a range of performance measures

Organisational control is the process of ensuring that an organisation is pursuing actions and strategies which will enable it to achieve its goals. The four unique characteristics of services cause problems in this area. The measurement and evaluation of performance are central to control, and mean posing three questions. What has happened? Why has it happened? What are we going to do about it? The essence of what we are proposing is that what one should measure depends on what one is trying to achieve. It is therefore a 'contingency theory' which argues that management information systems – which include management accounting systems – should vary according to a wide range of variables in which the chosen strategy should largely determine what is relevant. Such information, both financial and non-financial, should include feedforward control via plans, budgets, standards and targets, and feedback control by analysis of significant variances and the use of a range of performance measures, both competitor-based and customer-focused (see Figure 1.1). To be of use, feedback control must be a stimulus to appropriate *action* at the appropriate level of the organisation and stage of the decision-making process. Furthermore, the information supplied should vary according to the level of management and the stage of the decision-making process: there is a difference between information for diagnosis and information for control and performance measurement.

The selection of a range of performance measures in any service organisation must be made in the light of its strategic intentions, which

Figure 1.1: Feedforward: feedback control model

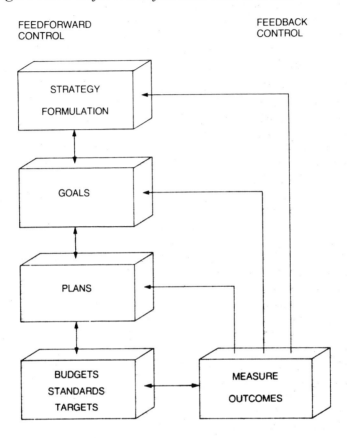

will have been formed to suit the competitive environment in which it operates and the kind of service business it is. If a company decides, for example, to differentiate itself in the market on the basis of service quality, then it should have measures in place to monitor and control service quality. If technological leadership and product innovation is the key source of a company's competitive advantage, then it should be measuring its performance in this area relative to its competitors. In contrast, companies competing primarily on price ('cost leaders') may tend to focus on measuring their resource utilisation and controlling costs.

In choosing a range of performance measures it will be necessary to balance them to ensure that one dimension of performance is not stressed to the excessive detriment of another. For example, a decision to upgrade quality may have a short-term adverse effect on profitability because of the costs incurred, but it may lead to greater customer loyalty and a long-term gain in market share and profits. An over-emphasis on short-term profitability might rule out such beneficial changes in strategy.

The dangers of focusing on short-term profit performance compared with budget are well known to management accountants. They include opportunistic management behaviour such as creative accounting, dysfunctional effects on quality and a failure to measure competitive performance. In one of several influential articles *Kaplan* claims that manufacturing industry is competing in areas such as quality, innovation and flexibility but that measures of performance in these areas are inadequate, inappropriate or unavailable:

'Perhaps the most damaging dysfunctional behaviour induced by short-term profit performance is the incentive . . . to reduce expenditures on discretionary and intangible investments. When profit targets become hard to achieve . . . managers try to minimise . . . expenditure on product and process development, promotion, distribution, quality improvement, applications engineering, human resources, customer relations and other intangibles' [8] (see also [9]).

These concerns apply equally to services, especially those which compete on quality. Since much of a service is intangible, it is difficult to measure performance: 'hard' measures such as profitability tend to drive out 'soft' measures like customer satisfaction, even though the intangible aspects of services may be important sources of competitive advantage. Monitoring the amount spent on them and their efficiency and effectiveness may be vital to competitive success.

Many authors from different management disciplines have claimed that performance measurement often focuses narrowly on easily quantifiable aspects such as cost and productivity, whilst neglecting other criteria which are important to competitive success [10].

We have synthesised their ideas into six generic performance dimensions:

- competitive performance;
- financial performance;
- quality of service;
- flexibility;
- resource utilisation;
- innovation.

It is important to realise that the six generic performance dimensions fall into two conceptually different categories. Measures of the first two, competitiveness and financial performance, reflect the success of the chosen strategy: 'ends' or 'results'. The other four are factors that *determine* competitive success: 'means' or 'determinants'. Table 1.1 overleaf shows some types of measures for each. Whereas all companies will wish to measure the results of their strategy, the mix of factors that determine their competitive success will vary. In consequence, whilst one would not expect much difference between companies' management accounting systems and use of competitiveness measures, one would anticipate systematic differences in their overall management information systems. Finally, measurement against this range of performance criteria may make visible the trade-offs which can exist between them: for example, trade-offs between short-term financial return and long-term competitive position, or between resource utilisation and service quality.

This type of approach to the design of a management information system will not of itself guarantee competitive success, but research confirms that this is what some successful service companies do.

1.4 An organising framework

The task of controlling service organisations may be usefully approached by viewing them in the terms of a simple input-process-output model, in which human and other resources flow through the process of designing, producing and delivering a service – what *Porter*[11] has called the 'value chain' (see Figure 1.2, page 10) through which companies create value for which customers are prepared to pay. Organisational performance on the six dimensions may be measured at any or all of these three stages. In Chapter 5, for example, it is shown that resource utilisation may be measured by comparing inputs to outputs. Such ratios could be in money or volume terms. Equally, as advocated in Chapter 2, costs can be collected in such a way that the process maps the value chain by which value is added throughout the service process.

Chapter 3 shows that quality may be measured at all three stages. For instance, customers may be involved at the input stage in determining the specification of the service to be supplied, as in the case of a management consultancy. During the process of a meal in a restaurant the head waiter should enquire whether everything is satisfactory. BAA use a market research organisation to sample customer satisfaction with service quality after the event.

Table 1.1: Performance measures across six dimensions

	DIMENSIONS OF PERFORMANCE	TYPES OF MEASURES
R **E** **S** **U** **L** **T** **S**	Competitiveness	Relative market share and position Sales growth Measures of the customer base
	Financial performance	Profitability Liquidity Capital structure Market ratios
D **E** **T** **E** **R** **M** **I** **N** **A** **N** **T** **S**	Quality of service	Reliability Responsiveness Aesthetics/appearance Cleanliness/tidiness Comfort Friendliness Communication Courtesy Competence Access Availability Security
	Flexibility	Volume flexibility Delivery speed flexibility Specification flexibility
	Resource utilisation	Productivity Efficiency
	Innovation	Performance of the innovation process Performance of individual innovations

A distinctive feature of the input-process-output model is that customers are often present during the service delivery process and are therefore in some sense both inputs to and outputs from the process: this distinguishes services from manufacturing and is a source of both threats and opportunities to service managers. The threats arise from the fact that, irrespective of their satisfaction with the service 'product', customers may not be happy with the process by which it is delivered and their treatment during it.

On the other hand, the presence of the customer in the process means there may be opportunities for cross-selling and allows corrective action to service quality during the service delivery process in response to customer feedback.

The simple input-process-output model does not reflect the wide differences in processes, mixes of inputs and types of output that may be found in a sample of real service organisations. *Fitzgerald et al.* [12] identified three different generic service types: *professional services, service shops* and *mass services.* We hope that they may become a common vocabulary by which managers in quite different service businesses may recognise that they share common problems, and that they may learn from each other. Although these archetypes of service business may span several different SIC service sectors, recognition that they nevertheless face common problems may lead to a cross-fertilisation of ideas for control and performance measurement. In particular the three-way typology may help to develop a range of performance measures across the six dimensions appropriate to each type of service.

The three service types were differentiated by *Fitzgerald et al.* in terms of the volume of customers processed by a typical unit per day against six other classification dimensions (see Figure 1.3, page 12)

- people/equipment focus
- front/back office focus
- product/process focus
- level of customisation of the service to any one customer
- discretion available to front office staff
- contact time available by front office staff

In this classification scheme the number of customers processed by a typical unit per day determines the volume of demand placed on the service business, and the other six classification dimensions detail aspects of the response to that demand.

The nature of the three archetypal service organisations is described below together with an example of each.

Professional Services

Professional services are defined as high-contact organisations where customers spend a considerable time in the service process. Such services provide high levels of customisation, the service process being highly adaptable in order to meet individual customer needs.

Figure 1.2: Input – process-output model.

Human resources

Customers

Other resources

INPUT

SERVICE PROCESS

* Inbound logistics
* Operations
* Outbound logistics
* Marketing and Sales
* After-sales service

OUTPUT

Tangible goods and services

Customers

Intangible services

A great deal of staff time is spent in the front office and contact staff are given considerable discretion in servicing customers. The amount of time and attention provided for each customer means that the ratio of staff to customers is high. The provision of professional service tends to be people-based rather than equipment-based. Emphasis is placed on the process (how the service is delivered) rather than the product (what is delivered). The large proportion of professional staff, the heterogeneity of tasks and the fuzziness of means-end relationships imply that employees be given greater autonomy: under these conditions organisational control is effected by short chains of command, and subjective organisational structure – shared values and culture – complements observable structure such as work group size and set procedures.

Exhibit 1.1 shows an example.

Exhibit 1.1 Professional service – management consultancy

Andersen Consulting sells the problem-solving expertise of its skilled staff to tackle clients' problems. Typically, the problem will first be discussed and the boundaries of a project defined. Each project is different. The project manager's role is to create a project team with the appropriate mix of skills to tackle the problem. A high proportion of work takes place at the client's premises, with frequent contact between members of the project team and the client.

Mass services

Mass services have many customer transactions, involving limited contact time and little customisation. Such services are predominantly equipment-based and product-orientated, with most value added in the back office and little judgement applied by front office staff. Here means-end relationships are clear; the mainly non-professional staff have a closely defined division of labour and follow set procedures.

Exhibit 1.2 Mass service – British Rail

British Rail moves large numbers of passengers with a variety of rolling stock on an immense infrastructure of railways. Passengers pick a journey from the range offered. British Rail ticket-office staff can advise passengers on the quickest or cheapest way to get from A to B, but they cannot 'customise' the service by putting on a special train for them.

Figure 1.3: Service classification scheme

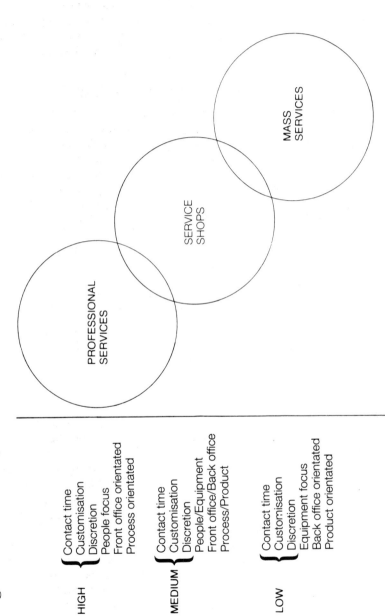

HIGH
- Contact time
- Customisation
- Discretion
- People focus
- Front office orientated
- Process orientated

MEDIUM
- Contact time
- Customisation
- Discretion
- People/Equipment
- Front office/Back office
- Process/Product

LOW
- Contact time
- Customisation
- Discretion
- Equipment focus
- Back office orientated
- Product orientated

PROFESSIONAL SERVICES

SERVICE SHOPS

MASS SERVICES

Low — High

Number of customers processed by a typical unit per day

Service shops

Service shops are characterised by levels of customer contact, customisation, volumes of customers and staff discretion which position them between the extremes of professional and mass services. Service is provided by means of mixes of front and back office activities, people and equipment, and of product/process emphasis.

Exhibit 1.3 Service shop – Multibroadcast Rental

Multibroadcast offers both rental and retail of home electronic products, with the former being predominant. A range of up-to-date products is offered with an emphasis on encouraging customers to trade-up to new models and new products. Front office staff have some technical training and can advise customers during the process of selling the product: they are not there solely to take the money. Essentially the customer is buying a product but will be influenced by the process of the sale.

Obviously, not all companies will necessarily fit neatly into one exclusive category. Hybrids exist, and any company may change over time as a result of strategic choice. Having said this, these generic differences, the degree of competition and the relative intangibility, heterogeneity, simultaneity and perishability of their services, will affect the problems faced by their managers, and accordingly will influence organisational strategies and the kinds of control systems and performance measures needed to ensure competitive success.

1.5 Conclusion

Empirical evidence suggests that some service managers are addressing the challenge of developing a range of measures to monitor the performance of their strategic business units. Strategic planning and control are just as much continual activities as day-to-day operations, but both are linked to the input-process-output model of delivering a daily service to customers. Service organisations need a balanced range of performance measures linked to the type of service they are delivering, their competitive environment and their chosen strategy for gaining and retaining a competitive advantage. In Chapters 2 to 6 we develop the six performance dimensions more fully, linking them to examples from the three generic service types. The aim is to provide sample measures of the six dimensions for each of the three service types (see Table 1.2 overleaf).

Table 1.2: Template of performance measures for three service archetypes

DIMENSIONS OF PERFORMANCE	TYPES OF SERVICE ORGANISATION		
	PROFESSIONAL	SERVICE SHOP	MASS
COMPETITIVENESS			
FINANCIAL PERFORMANCE			
QUALITY OF SERVICE			
FLEXIBILITY			
RESOURCE UTILISATION			
INNOVATION			

1.6 Key points

- This book is about performance measures which will help service industries devise and implement strategies to give them a sustainable competitive advantage.

- The three service types, professional services, service shops and mass services, compete on many dimensions so they need a range of performance measures linked to their competitive strategy.

- There are six generic performance dimensions split between two which measure the *results* of competitive success and four which measure factors that *determine* competitive success.

- All companies will wish to measure their results, but the mix of factors used to gain a competitive advantage will vary; as a consequence, measures of results will be similar across companies but measures of determinants may not.

- Use of a range of performance measures may make the need for trade-offs between them visible and so facilitate management choice between them.

- The control of operations and the implementation of strategy can be delegated and understood, using a simple input-process-output model.

References

[1] Johnston R., 'Service Industries – Improving Competitive Performance', *The Service Industry Journal*, Vol.8, No. 2, April 1988

[2] Quinn J.B. and Gagnon C.E., 'Will Services follow Manufacturing into Decline?', *Harvard Business Review*, November-December 1986

[3] Parasuraman A., Zeithaml V.A. and Berry L.L., 'A conceptual model of service quality and its implications for future research', *Journal of Marketing*, Fall 1985

[4] Berliner C. and Brimson J.A. (eds), *Cost Management for Today's Advanced Manufacturing*, Harvard Business School Press, 1988

[5] Day G. and Wensley R., 'Assessing Advantage: A Framework for Diagnosing Competitive Superiority', *Journal of Marketing*, July 1988

[6] Peters T. and Waterman R., *In Search of Excellence*, Harper & Row, 1982

[7] Shapiro A.C., 'Corporate Strategy and the Capital Budgeting Decision', reprinted in Stern and Chew (eds), *The Revolution in Corporate Finance*, Prentice Hall, 1986

8   Kaplan R.S., 'The Evolution of Management Accounting', *The Accounting Review*, Vol LIX, No 3, 1984b

9   Kaplan R.S., 'Measuring Manufacturing Performance: A New Challenge for Accounting Research', *The Accounting Review*, Vol LVII, No 4, 1983

10 Sink D.S., *Productivity Management: Planning, Measurement and Evaluation, Control and Improvement*, John Wiley 1985

11 Porter M., *Competitive Strategy*, Free Press, 1980 and *Competitive Advantage*, Free Press, 1985

12 Fitzgerald L., Johnston R. and Silvestro R., 'A Classification of Service Businesses', *Warwick Papers in Management*.

2
Measuring Results

'... a fundamental choice does need to be made. Management accountants may feel that their own area of comparative advantage is to measure, collect, aggregate, and communicate financial information. This will remain a valuable mission. But it is not likely a goal that will be decisive to the success of their own organisations, and if senior managers place too much emphasis on managing by the financial numbers, the organisation's long-term viability may become threatened.'

Kaplan R.S., 'The Evolution of Management Accounting', *The Accounting Review*, Vol. LIX, No. 3, 1984, p.414

2.1 Introduction

In Chapter 1 we introduced six generic performance dimensions and argued that, whereas two were results of competitive success, the other four were determinants thereof. This chapter looks at ways of measuring the two dimensions of results, but is not intended to over-emphasise their importance relative to measuring determinants.

A suggested framework for building and routinely monitoring competitive advantage, with particular relevance to our two dimensions of results, is that proposed by *Day* and *Wensley* [1] (see Figure 2.1 overleaf).

They argue that companies may build and maintain a competitive advantage in two ways: by focusing on the needs of customers, or by making comparisons with significant competitors. Ideally they should do both. A conclusion from *Day* and *Wensley's* work is that customers may be consulted when trying to measure the results of competitive success, but what determines those results largely depends on comparisons with competitors. Consequently, relevant measures of competitive and financial performance will embrace both competitor-based and customer-focused approaches.

2.2 Competitiveness

In Chapter 1 it was stressed that focusing on short-term financial performance might lead to neglect of the determinants of competitive success. One reason for advocating the measurement of results using

Figure 2.1: A framework for assessing advantage

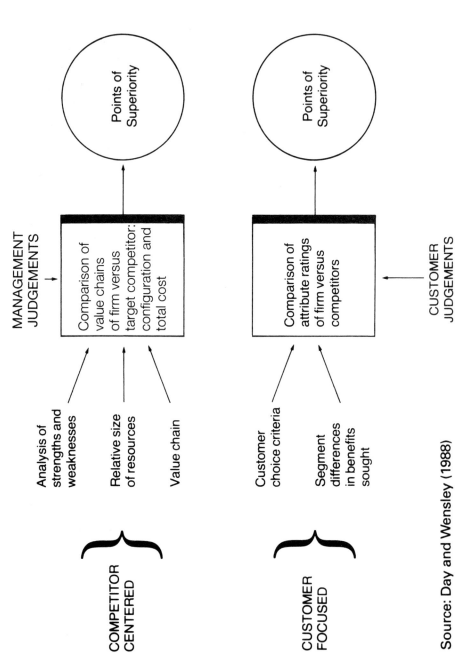

Source: Day and Wensley (1988)

competitive measures such as sales growth and market share, is that they should give extra information which may confirm or deny the financial results. More importantly, they may sometimes be better predictors of *future* short- to medium-term results than the latest annual historical cost earnings. This is because of the nature of the historical cost accounting (HCA) model, under which annual earnings are an estimate of long-run steady-state earning power, based on the twin assumptions that the past period's transactions are replicated at their historical costs. Assuming accurate and unbiased estimates, this means that HCA earnings are a good benchmark from which to estimate future earnings, as adjusted in the light of expectations about such factors as future sales volumes, prices and costs relative to the past. In this context, therefore, measures of competitiveness are useful because they may give early information on these factors, which will be reflected in earnings only after a time-lag.

Table 2.1 overleaf provides examples of competitiveness measures for different types of service business; a professional service – Andersen Consulting; a service shop – Commonwealth Hotels; and a mass service – a chain of newsagents. The measures in Table 2.1 include both competitor-based and customer-focused measures.

2.3 Financial performance

Conventional financial analysis distinguishes four types of ratio: *profitability*, *liquidity*, *capital structure* and *market* ratios. Analysis of a company's performance using accounting ratios involves comparisons with past trends and/or competitors' ratios. As is well known, such time-series and cross-sectional analyses are problematical [2]. Broadly, the problems fall into three categories.

(1) Choice of accounting policies

The flexibility of generally accepted accounting principles gives managers considerable choice in accounting policies adopted. Different companies may adopt different policies which will distort cross-sectional analyses. Individual companies may change their accounting policies over time which will distort time-series comparisons.

(2) Inflation

The distorting effects of inflation on historical costs in general and the variability of the impact of inflation on different companies will distort both time-series and cross-sectional data.

Table 2.1: Competitiveness measures and mechanisms

	PROFESSIONAL Andersen Consulting	SERVICE SHOP Commonwealth Hotels	MASS SERVICE Newsagents Chain
MEASURES			
Customer-focused	Repeat business	Repeat booking	Number of customers
Competitor-focused	Analysis of success/ failure of project tendering	Market share relative to competitors	Competitor's prices and product ranges
MECHANISMS			
Customer-focused	Partners' records	Customer survey	Customer survey
Competitor-focused	Partners' records	Comparison of occupancy ratios and room rates	Competitor surveys

(3) Comparison with industry standards

There may be difficulties in interpreting the significance of deviations in a company's ratios from some standard industry comparator or average, because the ratios of individual companies in an industry are unlikely to conform to a normal distribution.

In addition to traditional accounting ratio analysis, a company's financial performance may be examined by comparison with budgets as part of the feedback control process. Where a service firm faces a complex, uncertain environment, behavioural considerations suggest that use of a budget-constrained style of accounting information will be dysfunctional. The best use of budgets may be as a co-ordinating device and an aid to organisational learning: in other words, as an agent of *change*. As well as using budgets, firms may also ascertain the profitability of individual services by the accurate tracing of costs, and the comparison of actual costs with standards.

The preparation of *flexed* budgets, where actual numbers of customers compared with budget will affect the degree of flexing necessary, makes it easier to judge whether actual performance is better or worse than expected, and whether variances are the result of a flawed plan, or of good or bad implementation of the plan, or caused by unforeseen or uncontrollable external influences. Many services, however, have cost structures dominated by fixed costs, whether of capital or labour. Here there may be little to be gained from flexing the budget. In either event, the skilled interpretation of variances is a necessary step in the selection of appropriate action to complete the link between feedforward and feedback control loops.

Consideration of the financial performance of the manager of a sub-unit of an organisation, such as a division or a retail branch, is complicated by the need to distinguish between what is controllable by him and what is not. It is also vital to be clear whether one is measuring the performance of the manager or the sub-unit, for if one wishes to appraise the performance of the unit the emphasis switches from *controllable* assets, costs and revenues to *traceable* assets, costs and revenues. We focus here on the problems of running Strategic Business Units (SBUs), where an SBU is defined as an operating unit which sells a distinct set of products or services to an identifiable group of customers in competition with a defined set of organisations. For an SBU the business is given and the manager's task is to select a strategy to beat the competition while satisfying organisational performance requirements. For each of the three generic service types it is therefore necessary to be clear what the level of analysis is, and to ensure that assets, costs and revenues are accurately attached to each SBU.

Professional services are people-based and have a high traceability of costs and revenues to customers and services. Mass services are equipment-based and will have poor traceability of costs; even tracing revenues may be problematical. These factors will lead to systematic differences in cost structure, both in terms of fixed to variable cost, and labour to equipment cost. This will affect the way in which a given level of *profitability* would be earned. Whilst Return On Investment (ROI) is the fundamental profitability ratio, it is made up of two principal subsidiary ratios: Return On Sales and Asset Turnover. Mass services will tend to have lower asset turnover than professional services, but may or may not have a higher sales margin. As a result, whilst it might be reasonable to set the same ROI target for two divisions or SBUs operating in different service industries – if they both have the same degree of systematic risk – the way in which they reach it may, and perhaps should, differ. These facts might be acknowledged by setting appropriate targets for the two sub-components of ROI. In doing so it would be well to bear in mind the defects of ROI and other ratios derived from historical cost accounts, for reasons outlined earlier in this chapter.

2.4 Cost traceability

Since there are no good reasons why the use of liquidity, capital structure or market ratios should vary systematically across the three generic service types, the remainder of this chapter concentrates on the major financial variable which *will* vary systematically: the traceability of costs.

In general, costs may be used to plan, control and make decisions in organisations, but their mode of calculation should change according to the intended use. When we looked at a range of service companies we were surprised to find that many of them did not seem to try to accurately cost individual services, either to ascertain their profitability or to set prices. This may be explained by the difficulty many of them had in tracing costs, which varied systematically across the three service types.

We believe that cost traceability should match the input-process-output model shown in Chapter 1. At present most conventional costing systems concentrate on tracing inputs to outputs because information of this kind is needed for stock valuation in the financial accounts. Most management reporting systems do not focus on why and how costs are incurred in the functional activities of the firm, but the study of such costs could make an important contribution to planning and controlling all three types of service businesses.

The cost structures of professional services are dominated by labour costs. Such costs are easily traceable to individual jobs: for example, at management consultants' and solicitors' offices a simple diary system is operated in which professionals' chargeable time is booked to jobs, and non-chargeable time to training, holidays, sickness, and so on (see Figure 2.2 for the system at Andersen Consulting). As a result costs may be, and are, used to inform pricing decisions. Having relatively few

Figure 2.2: Andersen Consulting

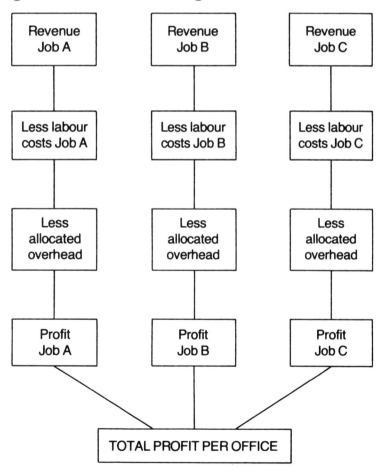

clients and jobs the setting of prices and the control of financial performance in such services are fairly straightforward, and may be facilitated by the use of conventional budgetary control. Resource utilisation may be more problematic, for although there will often be a predictable base workload, new clients and 'rush jobs' will have to be fitted in. Nevertheless, the management problems in professional services are probably more closely linked to quality, flexibility and innovation issues in the search for a sustainable competitive advantage. Recent examples of successful innovation in management consultancy are the growth of Strategy Consultants (for example Bain & Co) and the promotion of Activity-Based-Costing (ABC) by Peat Marwick consultants in conjunction with Harvard academics Robert Kaplan and Robin Cooper.

Cost traceability is more difficult in service shops, and in mass services it is a major management problem requiring widespread allocation if estimates of the profitability of individual services are required. The problem is the traceability of costs where there are multiple, heterogeneous and joint, inseparable services, compounded by the fact that individual customers may consume different mixes of services and may take different routes through the service process. A service shop example is the retail arm of Barclays Bank.

Exhibit 2.1 Service shop – Barclays Bank plc

Barclays Bank has segmented its business between corporate and retail customers. The bank has over 350 products and services, most of which are variants on borrowing or lending, whose profitability is tied to inter-bank borrowing and lending rates as affected by transactions with the Bank of England and government economic policy. Individual retail customers can consume a mix of these services – albeit in most cases a limited sample of the total range – via several possible service delivery processes: by post, telephone, automatic teller machines (ATMs), cashiers or the branch manager. Whilst the gross margins of individual services are known, no attempt is made to trace costs, even labour costs, to them (see Figure 2.3 opposite).

At the time of our investigation managerial effort at branch level was devoted to raising service quality and resource utilisation, particularly via staff flexibility, whilst efforts were made at regional and headquarters levels to gain market share and competitive advantage through back-

Figure 2.3: Barclays Bank plc

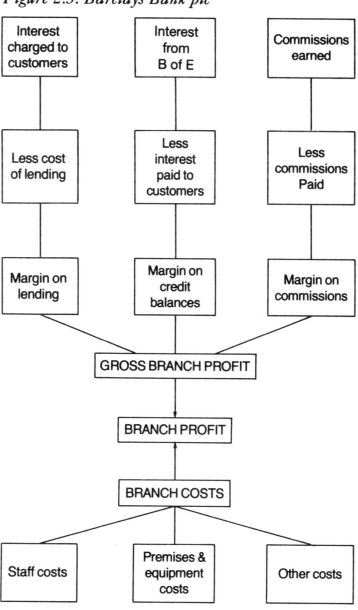

office innovation. Financial control was exercised via profitability targets at 'responsibility centres' – individual branches and regions. Costs were used for planning and controlling, but not to make pricing decisions. Individual services are merely part of the package and the aim is to maximise the profitability of the package as a whole, not individual parts of it. There is a problem here, however, since the organisation is treating the individual branch as though it is one SBU. In fact it is two SBUs, serving two different markets: corporate and retail. It is not just the customers who vary here: the services offered and the competition faced are different too. For example, in recent years the clearing banks have encountered competition in the retail banking market from the newly deregulated building societies, but the latter do not compete in the corporate banking market.

Barclays' corporate arm is offering a professional service, whilst the retail operation is a classic service shop. Structured in this way, the organisation was not collecting assets, costs and revenues around each SBU, and so could not evaluate the financial performance of either. In particular, the possibility of using a diary system to trace labour costs to corporate clients and services was being neglected.

In practice Barclays also had a long way to go in developing a balanced range of performance measures, although it has since made significant progress in this direction. At the time of our investigation it had numerous measures of branch financial performance and resource utilisation, but despite its claim to be competing on a strategy of differentiation by service quality it had few quality measures, and none at all for flexibility or innovation. This may reflect the relatively recent increase in competition in high street banking, which may have outstripped the bank's ability to change its organisational culture.

Exhibit 2.2 Service shop – Commonwealth Hotels

A similar yet different situation was observed at Commonwealth Hotels International. Each hotel (an SBU) had a general manager and a number of responsibility centres: rooms, food, bar, reception (including telephones) and marketing. Individual customers could consume any mix of these services. Here gross margins (after deducting all direct costs) were known, but indirect costs were not allocated to the responsibility centres (see Figure 2.4 opposite). As a result the information was there to undertake marginal cost pricing to maximise the use of fixed capacity, and the management *team* was rewarded by a bonus system related to the hotel's *total* profit.

Figure 2.4: Commonwealth Hotels International Co.

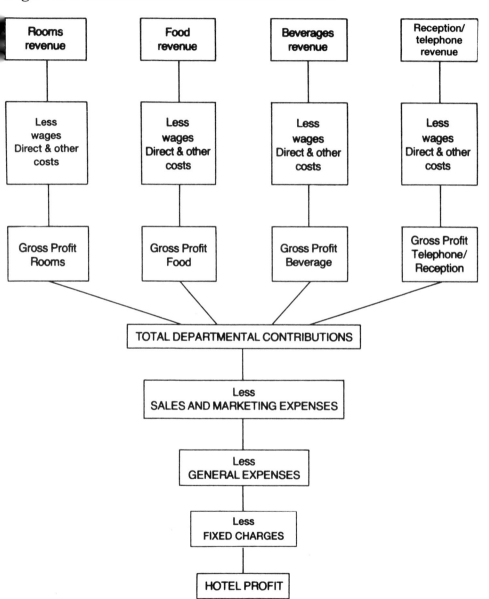

In this case costs were used to plan and control the SBU via responsibility centres which, in *Porter's* terms, constituted its 'value chain' [3] via which the hotel added value to its services. This contrasts with the situation at Barclays, where costs were not broken down in the branch along the value chain for planning and control purposes, nor did they separate the assets and costs of the two SBUs. In such service shop businesses, however, it is often not apparent how the attributes that are important to the customer are influenced by activities in the value chain. In securing a competitive advantage we would therefore expect, using *Day* and *Wensley's* framework (see above), that the companies would not just look at their competitors but also use performance measures at the SBU level which are 'customer-focused', including customer satisfaction surveys, estimates of customer loyalty, relative share of end-user segments, and so on. Commonwealth Hotels successfully combined such measures with competitor comparisons.

Exhibit 2.3 Mass service – British Rail

An example of a mass service is British Rail.

Whilst it has eight SBUs, the primary task of the company is to move passengers from their starting point, A, to B, which might be anywhere in Great Britain and involve a short journey or a long one, with or without a change of train in between. British Rail's network structure is quite complicated:

(1) Many items of rolling stock supply capacity jointly to more than one SBU during a day.

(2) A passenger's demand for a train journey on any route (other than a short local journey) is actually a joint demand by many passengers for a chain of permanent-way capacity.

(3) Much rolling stock within each SBU is not dedicated to a particular route but is utilised by different routes at different times.

In an effort to cope with this complexity BR undertakes extensive cost and revenue allocations within and between its eight different SBUs as an aid to a complicated pricing structure which varies according to route, time of day, and other factors (see Figure 2.5 opposite). This is in turn linked to capacity planning: capacity management is a major management problem in mass services because of their significant fixed infrastructure costs, and BR is no exception to this.

Figure 2.5: British Rail

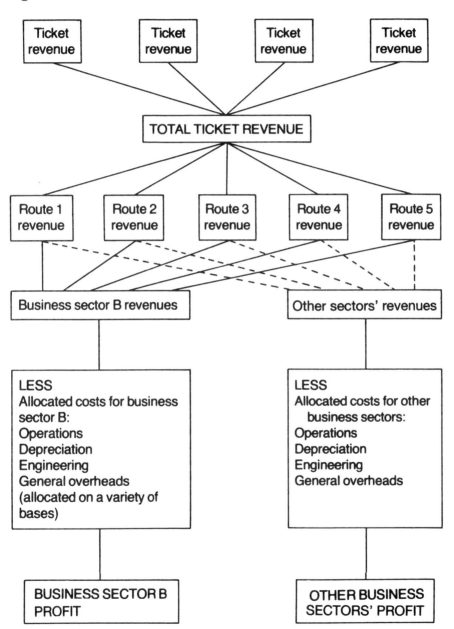

2.5 Conclusion

In Chapter 1 it was argued that one would expect few significant differences between companies' management accounting systems, measuring financial performance. Table 2.2 on p.32 shows some measures of two of the four types of financial performance ratio for examples of each of the three generic services. At the SBU level capital structure and market ratios are not used.

In practice the major difference identified was in the *use of costing*. Costs are not extensively used to make pricing decisions in service industries except in professional services. They are, however, extensively used to plan and control via responsibility centres, often linked to the problem of capacity management. These roles might be enhanced by more closely aligning responsibility centres with an organisation's value chain [4] having first ensured that assets, costs and revenues are being attached to each SBU. Equally, the use of more accurate costing methods such as ABC would be justified where the expected benefits outweighed the expected costs [5]. These two moves would give service industries attention-directing information about which services make demands on which responsibility centres and functional departments. ABC attaches indirect costs more accurately to individual services and customers. Value chain analysis (VCA) focuses control on all the value chain through a knowledge of which of *Porter's* ten 'cost drivers' affects the behaviour of each item of cost, such as economies of scale, pattern of capacity utilisation, and discretionary policies, such as level of service. Both ABC and VCA give information for strategy formation, evaluation and adjustment at the SBU level.

These ideas (ABC and VCA) are especially applicable to mass services and service shops with heterogeneous outputs, many customers, heavy investment in equipment and high levels of indirect and fixed costs. Here the real cost-driving forces are diversity, complexity and (of course) the degree of competitive pressure. Where these factors apply to a company it should not only examine its own performance, but those of its principal competitors. The study of competitors' cost structures and the likely relative fluctuations of unit costs when demand varies may be an important weapon in the search for a *sustainable* competitive advantage.

Most of the service industries we observed were competing via some form of differentiation strategy, whilst also keeping an eye on costs. Accountants can play a useful role in strategy formation by costing the differentiating attributes and subsequently monitoring and reporting on these costs. Equally, as relative cost structure may determine whether an advantage is sustainable, it is important to report 'sunk' infrastructure costs (past capital expenditures still present on the balance sheet and being amortised as annual charges to the profit and loss account) as they may represent significant barriers to entry into the industry [6]. Barriers to entry may tend to be higher for mass services than for the other two archetypes.

2.6 *Key points*

- Measures of competitive and financial performance should include both competitor-based and customer-focused measures.

- There are no good reasons why the use of measures of competitive performance should vary across the three generic service types. This is also true of three of the four traditional financial performance ratios: liquidity, capital structure and market ratios.

- The make-up of the fourth financial performance ratio, profitability, will vary across the three service types because of their different cost structures.

- Cost traceability affects the extent to which costs can be used to plan, control and make decisions in organisations, and cost collection should be done in three ways to match our input-process-output model: to inputs, to outputs and to the functional activities of the firm. Professional services have high cost traceability, mass services low cost traceability.

- Only professional services appear to use costs routinely for pricing decisions. All services use costs for planning and controlling their organisations; in mass services and service shops this is often linked to strategies aimed at maximising the utilisation of fixed capacity.

- The use of costs to plan and control would be aided if functional responsibility centres were aligned with the organisation's value chain. Activity based costing is worth consideration for attention-directing, but its cost might outweigh its benefits. Both VCA and ABC are likely to be especially useful to mass services and service shops characterised by diversity and complexity and operating in highly competitive markets.

- Relative cost structure is an important determinant of sustainable competitive advantage. It is therefore necessary to ensure that assets, costs and revenues are accurately attached to SBUs in order that cost structure and profitability comparisons can be made with significant competitors.

Table 2.2: Financial Measures

DIMENSIONS OF PERFORMANCE	PROFESSIONAL Andersen Consulting	SERVICE SHOP Multibroadcast Rentals	MASS SERVICE BAA plc
PROFITABILITY	Profit Value of outstanding work in progress	Profit Contribution per rental asset	Profit Return on Net Assets
LIQUIDITY	Debtor days Credit days	Working capital	Working capital
CAPITAL STRUCTURE	NA	NA	NA
MARKET RATIOS	NA	NA	NA

References

[1] Day G. and Wensley R., 'Assessing Advantage: A Framework for Diagnosing Competitive Superiority', *Journal of Marketing*, July 1988

[2] Foster G., *Financial Statement Analysis*, 2nd edition, Prentice Hall, 1986

[3] Porter M., *Competitive Strategy*, Free Press, 1980 and *Competitive Advantage*, Free Press, 1985

[4] Hergert M. and Morris D., 'Accounting Data for Value Chain Analysis', *Strategic Management Journal*, Vol. 10, 1989

[5] Cooper R. and Kaplan R.S., 'Measure Costs Right: Make the Right Decisions', *Harvard Business Review*, September-October 1988

[6] Bromwich M., 'The Case for Strategic Management Accounting: The Role of Accounting Information for Strategy in Competitive Markets', *Accounting, Organisations and Society*, Vol. 15, No. 1/2, 1990

3
Measuring Service Quality

'Service quality is more difficult to measure than product quality. In service industries such as consulting, advertising, hotels, transportation, banks, insurance, Government and tourism, it's hard to tell when you are doing a good job.'

The *Wall Street Journal*, 30 December 1986

3.1 Service quality – a competitive weapon

As customers of service organisations we often feel that we have received poor treatment. Indeed, some service organisations seem to be run with the object of causing as little inconvenience to their staff as possible. Nevertheless, many organisations, both manufacturing and service, are recognising that by improving their level of service they can make significant and sustainable gains in the marketplace. Service quality can be, and increasingly is, a competitive weapon.

For manufacturing and product-orientated organisations, service quality may be an important means of differentiation if they are operating in markets where there is little product differentiation or where product development may be slow, difficult, expensive or short-lived. Service quality – the way the products are provided for the customer or additional services which the customer receives – may be a means to competitive success. Exhibit 3.1 describes a UK brewery, a product-orientated organisation, that realised the importance of service quality.

Exhibit 3.1 Crisis in the brewing industry

In 1987 the public house trade was facing a crisis. People were spending less and less in public houses in the UK, not only because of the current economic recession but also as a result of increasing pressures to reduce the nation's consumption of alcohol. Each company in the industry was having to work hard just to maintain its share of a slowly declining market. Many attempts were made by the breweries to deal with the situation, from divestment to changing public houses into eating houses, from increasing the range of products to improving the appeal of pubs to certain market segments. The situation was expected to become even more difficult, as the population of 18- to 30-year-olds, the majority of drinkers, was starting to decline.

A senior manager, responsible for staff training and development at one UK brewery, had some firm ideas as to how the company could face this crisis. He said, 'There is a need for any brewery that is to survive in the beer, wine and spirit retail trade to be able to differentiate itself from the competition. This is not an easy task as all our competitors have similar locations, with similar products at similar prices. Even when a competitor brings out a new product, it is relatively easy for us or anyone else to reproduce it at similar prices. The problem is that the company does not have a unique selling point. There is nothing that differentiates us from the competition.'

'One factor that I believe is the underlying key to success is based on the observation that the volume of trade in a pub does not seem to be too closely related to products or promotions or to market strengths or weaknesses, but is very much dependent upon the licensed house manager (LHM), his or her attributes, abilities and the way he or she runs the pub. I believe that seeking a competitive edge through service as opposed to products could have a substantial impact on volume. I really believe that we should differentiate ourselves by concentrating our time and efforts on the way the service is provided; how the customer is dealt with.'

'You may argue that good customer service is equally as reproducible as products. However, I believe that to achieve real and lasting service improvement is relatively difficult and requires changes not only in the pub itself but to overall company culture and central control systems. This I believe could be difficult for a less forward looking and flexible company to follow.'

Service-orientated companies too, are recognising that there may be a need to provide high levels of customer service. Increasing competition, declining sales and more service-aware customers are putting pressure on service organisations to rethink and improve the levels of service that they offer. For example, Jan Carlzon, the chief executive and president of Scandinavian Airline Systems (SAS), implemented a strategy of significantly increasing the level of service provided by his company in the two years between 1981 and 1983. During the late 1970s the airline business was becoming highly competitive as the recent growth in the intercontinental market had stagnated and recent oil crises had pushed up operating costs. By 1981, SAS had a poor reputation. It had been making a loss for two years, had low productivity, over-capacity, poor punctuality and overall a poor service image. Carlzon was concerned that his management seemed to be too busy flying aeroplanes and were not concerned with the quality of the customers' experience. SAS had lost its understanding and awareness of the customer. Carlzon's job was to improve the quality of service to attract more full-fare-paying passengers. In Exhibit 3.2 Jan Carlzon describes the situation and how he saw the role of service quality.

Exhibit 3.2 Service quality at SAS

'At SAS we used to think of ourselves as the sum total of our aircraft, our maintenance bases, our offices and our administrative procedures. But if you ask our customers about SAS they won't tell you about our planes or our offices or the way we finance our capital investments. Instead they'll talk about their experiences with people at SAS. SAS is not just a collection of material assets but also, and even more importantly, the quality of contact between an individual customer and the SAS employees who service the customer directly. Last year, each of our ten million customers came into contact with approximately five SAS employees and this contact lasted an average of fifteen seconds each time. Thus, SAS is "created" in the minds of our customers 50 million times a year, fifteen seconds at a time. These 50 million "moments of truth" are the moments that ultimately determine whether SAS will succeed or fail as a company. They are the moments when we must prove to our customers that SAS is the best alternative.' [1]

Service quality for Jan Carlzon was about improving the treatment of customers throughout the service process. By understanding the needs of the business traveller, and identifying all the aspects of the service that were important to him/her, Carlzon was able to devise a strategy to enable his staff to provide such a service. Two years later, SAS had become one of the most punctual in Europe and number one choice for Scandinavian business executives. It was back in the black and in 1983 won Fortune's Airline of the Year Award for 'Overall excellence and outstanding service to the customers'.

3.2 Service quality defined

Jan Carlzon knew that service quality was not only about having the right products (routes) and the right facilities (aircraft), it was about making sure that the whole of the customer's experience was right. Service quality refers to the quality of the entire service package: the goods – the tangible, physical objects that are used within the service system or removed from it by the customer; the environment where the service takes place; and the service provided, that is the treatment of the customer or of the things belonging to the customer.

Some service organisations have taken a much narrower view of service quality as epitomised by the 'have a nice day' syndrome. Whilst this insincere and tired phrase may form an essential ingredient in the rigid procedures of some service organisations, it belies and belittles the notion of providing a quality service, which is to ensure the provision of quality with all aspects of the service.

Service quality is the totality of features and characteristics of the service package that bear upon its ability to satisfy a customer need.

This is a market-based definition of service quality, based on the need for service organisations to be customer orientated and on the premise that their role is that of satisfying customer requirements, whether the customer is internal to the organisation, or external to it. Whilst organisations may control and measure quality internally, it is the degree of fit between a customer's expectation of the level of service to be delivered and his/her perceptions of the level of service provided which is paramount[2.]

The process of improving service quality is recognised as a difficult activity, and often requires changes to organisational culture, control systems, training activities and possibly even recruitment activities. It was the UK brewery's inability to change its culture and control systems that, in the end, prevented it from improving the level of service it provided. The fact that the organisation remained product-orientated is epitomised by its unwillingness to change making deliveries to a busy office pub at lunchtime on Fridays. In addition, its burdensome financial control systems not only kept the licensed house managers away from the bar so that they could not manage the 'moments of truth' and lead their staff from the front, but were so exacting that the control systems seemed to imply that the managers were cheats and thieves! This situation was not particularly conducive to the provision of high-quality service.

Whilst Total Quality Management (TQM) is outside the scope of this study, this chapter deals with one important plank of TQM, the measurement of service quality. The first stage is to identify and define the characteristics that a service must have in order to meet customers' needs and expectations.

3.3 Characteristics of service quality

At SAS, Jan Carlzon used market research to identify the features or characteristics that bore upon his organisation's ability to satisfy business passengers. Punctuality was found to be one of the most important. Also included was the time of arrival, seating comfort, space to work, the range of newspapers, food and drinks, the distance that had to be travelled in the airport between connections as well as the number of connections necessary to make a journey.

Service quality, therefore, is a multi-factor phenomenon. Customers' expectations are rarely concerned with a single aspect of the service package but with many of them. This creates two difficulties for service managers. First, the many different characteristics of service quality have to be monitored and controlled. Second, different customers will have different expectations (referred to in Chapter 1 as heterogeneity). For example, whilst the business executive travelling by train may see peace, solitude and space to work as important factors during the journey, these ideals may not be shared by the person opposite going on holiday, who may hope for conversation and companionship. Furthermore, such expectations will vary not only from customer to customer but may also vary as situations change. An airline passenger's priority may be, at one moment, to arrive at the destination on time, making the punctuality of the service important, but if the aircraft develops engine trouble the arrival time is of little significance compared to a safe landing on the ground, anywhere, at any time!

An additional difficulty for the management and control of service quality is the intangible aspect of services. For instance, in an expensive restaurant the customer purchases, and has expectations about, not only the food, but many intangible elements: the presentation of the food, the attitude of the waiter and the ambience of the restaurant. Formulating clear and precise quality specifications for presentation, attitude and ambience may be difficult. As creating a quality specification is difficult, so too is measuring quality and setting targets against which a service can be controlled.

A research team in the United States identified ten factors or characteristics of service quality [3]. In earlier research [4] we identified, from both a customer and company perspective, twelve factors, or characteristics, pertaining to the service quality of both the tangible goods part of the service package and the intangible, 'service' part of the package, as well as the environment in which the service is delivered. Table 3.1 lists all twelve factors and illustrates the features relative to the tangible product, the service and the environment. Not all factors are applicable to the product, service and environmental parts of the package, e.g. courtesy refers only to the service, the interaction between staff and customers, and not to the products or environment.

The relative importance of each of the twelve factors illustrated in Table 3.1 vary according to the particular services and products provided, the nature of competition and a company's strategic intentions. To illustrate this, Exhibits 3.3, 3.4 and 3.5 contain descriptions of three organisations and a summary of the key quality service factors that their management considered to be important.

Exhibit 3.3 A firm of solicitors

A firm of solicitors in a small market town in the south west of England comprises two partners who had previously worked together in a large London firm. They both felt that London held few attractions and that they would prefer their own small country practice. Six years ago they moved to offices just off the town's high street and set up in competition with four other firms of solicitors. It was a slow start but both partners are now very busy and have a secretarial staff of five.

This professional service organisation has two distinct types of client. There is the personal client who is the local individual with a small legal problem, such as a house purchase or a boundary dispute, and there is the commercial client who is a company. A few of these are local but most are based in Bristol, Gloucester, Cheltenham, Bath or Cirencester.

The personal client is someone who comes through the door with a problem, tending to choose a solicitor through recommendation from friends. The partners have worked hard to build up their local clients. They use a personal approach and try to break down the stuffy image of the law and deal at a simple, straightforward level with the client. They see themselves as a small, local, convenient and friendly firm based on a good, personal and caring image.

The practice is chosen by commercial firms usually as a result of recommendation from other companies or by third parties like accountants. Sometimes jobs arrive through speculative phone calls from potential clients. The partners have expanded their business in this area by following up such calls quickly, initially over the phone, followed by a personal visit to the company.

Table 3.1: Illustrations of the service quality factors

QUALITY FACTOR	PRODUCT EXAMPLES	SERVICE EXAMPLES	ENVIRONMENTAL EXAMPLES
Access			convenience of unit location ease of finding way around clarity of route
Aesthetics/ Appearance	appearance of goods taste of | food	appearance of staff	appearance of facilities level of decor
Availability	product availability product range product variety	staff availability/ visibility facility availability	
Cleanliness/ Tidiness	of goods	of staff	of facilities
Comfort			of environment seating comfort atmosphere ambience congestion
Communication	intelligibility and clarity of product information	intelligibility and clarity of staff-customer interaction	clarity of sign-posting
Competence		staff skill, expertise, knowledge, thoroughness	
Courtesy		politeness respect propriety of staff towards customer	
Friendliness		helpfulness of staff attentiveness	
Reliability	product reliability	delivery reliability punctuality dependability of service dependability of staff	consistency of environment
Responsiveness		delivery speed response times	
Security	physical security product safety	confidentiality	personal security

Key service quality factors:

- *friendliness* – a personal and caring relationship with the client
- *access* – the convenience of the location for personal clients
- *responsiveness* – speed of follow-up and delivery for commercial clients

Exhibit 3.4 Multibroadcast Rental Ltd

This 'service shop' company is in the business of renting out equipment such as televisions, videos, microwaves and hi-fi systems. This accounts for about 90 per cent of its business; the remainder is concerned with equipment sales. In recent years the rental market had been in decline, mainly because of decreasing product costs and the increasing reliability of the equipment. Whilst the traditional focus for this company had been to try to increase the number of rented units, it was now emphasising rental margins and profit. The company directors considered that the key to improved profitability was to increase revenue per household and to retain existing customers. The company therefore was implementing a differentiation strategy based upon service quality and technological innovation. Shops were being refitted to convey an upmarket image and considerable investment was being made in the most up-to-date range of products.

Key service quality factors:

- *reliability* – reliability of the goods was a key means of maintaining customer loyalty

- *availability* – the availability of a range of technologically advanced goods was essential to maintain their competitive edge

- *aesthetics* – the pleasing appearance of the shop, the staff and the products

- *friendliness* – the friendliness of staff towards customers in the shop

Exhibit 3.5 BAA plc

BAA plc is an international airport group which was privatised in 1987. It is a 'mass service' organisation and owns and operates, through subsidiary companies, seven UK airports: Heathrow, Gatwick, Stanstead, Glasgow, Edinburgh, Prestwick and Aberdeen. BAA is in a virtual monopoly position, handling 75 per cent of air passengers and 85 per cent of air cargo tonnage in the UK.

BAA has little direct control over the volume of passengers it can attract to the airport. The main reasons for passengers' choice of airport are usually flight destinations and departure times, which are not determined by BAA but by the airlines and the Civil Aviation Authority.

BAA is concerned about the quality of its services for two reasons. First, it has identified a number of passengers who select airports on the basis of the facilities (in addition to the other decision criteria mentioned above), particularly travellers who use European airports to change flights, representing about 20 per cent of international users. BAA considers itself to be competing directly with other European airports for the custom of these passengers, and believes that by providing good facilities and high quality services it can play an active role in attracting them to its airports.

Second, when BAA was a nationalised industry it was obliged to publish certain non-financial indicators of performance in order to demonstrate to the sponsoring Government department that it was not achieving its financial objectives at the expense of business efficiency or service standards. Since privatisation the directive from the chairman of the company has been that BAA should continue to demonstrate to share-holders, customers and the general public, its concern to maintain high service levels as well as improve profit performance. Indeed, this is considered to be important for the protection of BAA's virtual monopoly position as a privatised airport group.

This being the case, one of BAA's mission statements is to 'constantly seek to improve the service we provide to our customers, including passengers, airlines and other airport users' (Annual Report and Accounts, 1988).

Key service quality factors:

- *communication* – the availability and clarity of information for passengers
- *availability* – the availability of staff and of equipment in working order
- *cleanliness/tidiness* – the cleanliness of the airport and its facilities
- *access* – the walking distances involved and the ease of finding one's way around the airport
- *comfort* – the comfort of the facilities and the levels of congestion

3.4 Service quality measures

Having identified the service quality factors for a service organisation, the next step is to measure performance in terms of these factors. Whilst some companies may measure only the key ones, others may measure and control all service quality factors. Again the choice in this matter is a function not only of customer needs but also of the strategic intentions and competitive positioning of the company.

Exhibit 3.6 describes not only the measures used by BAA plc, but also the mechanisms used to collect such information. Examples of the detailed measures and mechanisms for all twelve service quality factors used by the company are summarised in Table 3.2 opposite.

Exhibit 3.6 Service quality measures – BAA plc

BAA uses regular customer surveys for measuring customer perceptions of a wide variety of service quality attributes, including, for example, the cleanliness of its facilities, the helpfulness of its staff and the ease of finding one's way around the airport. Public correspondence is also analysed in detail, and comment cards are available in the terminals so that passengers can comment voluntarily on service levels received. Duty terminal managers also sample the services and goods offered by service outlets in the terminals, assessing them from a customer perspective. They check the cleanliness and condition of service facilities and complete detailed checklists which are submitted daily to senior terminal managers. The company has also a wealth of internal monitoring systems that record equipment faults and failures, and report equipment and staff availability. These systems are supported by the terminal managers who circulate the terminals on a full-time basis, helping customers as necessary, reporting any equipment faults observed and making routine assessments of the level of service provided by BAA and its concessionaires.

Assessing service quality using other performance measures

Whilst the means discussed and illustrated hitherto are measures of specific characteristics of service quality, it may also be assessed by monitoring the other measures of performance. Market-based measures are a frequently used indicator of service quality levels. For example, Multibroadcast uses the number of rental terminations in a given period compared to other periods, and the number of net gained or lost customers to indicate possible changes in its service quality. BAA uses the number of complaints per 100,000 passengers as an indicator of overall customer satisfaction with service quality. Many organisations use financial measures, especially profit, as an indicator of the possible effects of changes in service quality levels. Some organisations use resource

Table 3.2: Examples of service quality measures and mechanisms at BAA plc

SERVICE QUALITY FACTORS	MEASURES	MECHANISMS
Access	walking distances	customer survey and internal operational data
	ease of finding way around	customer survey
Aesthetics/ Appearance	staff appearance	customer survey
	airport's appearance	customer survey
	quantity, quality, appearance of food	management inspection
Availability	equipment availability	internal fault monitoring system & customer survey customer survey and internal operational data
Cleanliness/ Tidiness	cleanliness of environment and equipment	customer survey and management inspection
Comfort	crowdedness of airport	customer survey and management inspection
Communication	information clarity	customer survey
	clarity of labelling and pricing	management inspection
Competence	staff efficiency	management inspection
Courtesy	courtesy of staff	customer survey and management inspection
Friendliness	staff attitude and helpfulness	customer survey and management inspection
Reliability	number of equipment faults	internal fault monitoring systems
Responsiveness	staff responsiveness	customer survey
Security	efficiency of security checks	customer survey
	number of urgent safety reports	internal operational data

measures. For example, Barclays Bank uses its branch productivity index as a quality indicator, believing that if productivity becomes too high then quality of service is likely to be suffering. Solicitors use the proportion of time spent with clients as an indicator of quality. Management consultancy companies use supervisor/staff ratios, the percentage of time spent on recruitment and training and labour turnover as indicators of their likely quality levels. Multibroadcast uses labour turnover as a quality indicator. BAA uses a supervisor/staff ratio and a customer/staff ratio as indicators of likely quality levels.

Whilst these measures do not directly measure service quality per se, many organisations do use them as indicators of overall internal or external service quality.

3.5 Service quality measurement systems

This section describes the mechanisms, or systems, used by service companies for directly measuring service quality.

The measurement can be based on information collected from two different data sources. First, it can be measured internally, using the company's own internal control systems, e.g. BAA's fault monitoring systems. Second, it can be measured externally – a customer-focused approach – using customers' assessment of the level of service provided, for instance, through surveys and questionnaires. These internal and customer-focused measures may also be supported by competitor-focused measures. By being able to assess the internal quality levels or customer satisfaction levels of competitors, a company can provide itself with a benchmark for competitive positioning and improvement. Whilst at present, little competitor benchmarking takes place in the UK, it is relatively common practice in the USA.

Service quality, either external or internal, can be measured at the various stages in the service delivery process identified in Chapter 1, that is, at the input stage, during the process of service delivery, or after the service has been provided at the output stage. The remainder of this section provides examples of external and internal service quality mechanisms at all three stages. These have been summarised in Table 3.3.

External customer satisfaction measurement

The top half of Table 3.3 identifies the kinds of measurement systems that can be used to assess customer satisfaction with a service at various stages in the service system; whether at input stage, when customers may be involved, in some organisations, with the specification of the service to be provided, or during the process, or at the output stage when customers may assess the quality of the service after the event.

Table 3.3: Quality measurement systems at different stages in the service process

	INPUT	PROCESS	OUTPUT
External Customer Satisfaction Mechanisms	Customer Involvement With Specification	Customer Assessment During the Process	Customer Assessment After the Event
	negotiations of specification with customer	management sampling service mystery shoppers	surveys after-sales calls
Internal Quality Mechanisms	Internal Assessment Before Process	Internal Assessment During Process	Internal Assessment After the Event
	people/skills equipment, facility availability	management inspection monitoring equipment	internal monitoring systems

The firm of solicitors in Exhibit 3.3 involve their customers in negotiation of the service specification before they undertake the job. They discuss the legal problems with the client and the course of action that they propose to take on the client's behalf. Many consultancy companies, too, negotiate the specification of the service with the client to ensure that the quality specification is feasible and achievable.

Many service companies do not measure service quality during the process of delivery because the collection of such information, in some cases, may interfere with the process itself. Restaurants are one exception to this where head waiters are expected to check that 'everything is all right' during the meal. BAA use their duty terminal managers to sample some of the services of the airport from a customer's point of view. Other organisations, such as Multibroadcast, use more formal means and employ 'mystery shoppers'. These are 'customers' usually employed by an external agency to sample the service and report back to the management on how they were treated during the process of service delivery.

The outputs of the service may be measured by using surveys to assess customers' satisfaction with the service. Surveys may be conducted face to face, over the telephone or by post. BAA plc use the services of a market research organisation to sample customers and question their satisfaction with many aspects of the service, including ease of finding ways around, satisfaction with information and equipment availability. Multibroadcast have a system of ringing customers after the installation of equipment to check that they are satisfied with the result.

Internal quality measurement

Organisations, too, may measure their service performance from within. Again, quality may be checked before the event, during it or after, or by using overall indicators of service quality.

Inspection and monitoring of the inputs to the service process is important for all organisations. The quality of the solicitors in a practice or the number and grades of staff available in a consultancy organisation are crucial to the provision of service quality. Multibroadcast measure the number of shop refits per month and BAA monitor the availability and condition of equipment and facilities.

Many service companies use internal mechanisms to measure service quality during the process of service delivery. Multibroadcast use managers to formally inspect the premises, goods and service provided by the staff using detailed checklists covering, for example, the correct pricing of items, correct layout of displays and attitude of staff to the customers. BAA have advanced systems to monitor equipment faults and the terminal managers are expected to report any problems they see.

The quality of the service may be measured after the event, that is by measuring the results or outputs of the service. For example, Multibroadcast measure the number of service calls they have to make for each of their products, in order to assess product reliability.

3.6 Linking external and internal quality measurement

Many service organisations use a combination of internal and external quality measurements for three reasons: first, to facilitate the setting of service quality targets; second, to assess the cost sensitivity of changing quality targets; third, to allow the linking of managers' pay to service quality levels achieved.

(1) Target setting

One of the most common complaints at airports is the lack of baggage trolleys. If airport companies measured the availability of trolleys using only internal measures, the number of trolleys and trolley parks and the number of trolleys in each trolley park, it would tell only a part of the story. What is missing is a reading of customer satisfaction with trolley availability. If this is 97 per cent, for example, then the company knows the perceived quality level for a given level of resources. Likewise, if the number of satisfied customers is known but not the actual number of trolleys, management has insufficient information to help it make decisions. Internal and external quality data are therefore required to allow a company to assess customer satisfaction with a part of the service package, given a known level of resources. Armed with these two pieces of information about a particular part of the service, the organisation can then create meaningful quality targets. For example, an airport terminal company may accept that 97 per cent satisfaction is a suitable target for satisfaction with trolley availability. It may wish, however, to improve its quality to 98 per cent satisfaction with the service. In that case it may have to consider purchasing equipment, hiring staff or redesigning the service process.

(2) Cost sensitivity of changing quality targets

As well as setting targets, the company may be able to test the cost sensitivity of changing such targets. If the airport wished to improve customers' satisfaction with trolley availability to 99 per cent, it could buy more trolleys and employ more people to move them from the car parks to the terminal building or vice versa. Whatever its tactic, the effect could be monitored in terms of customer satisfaction. This would reveal whether that tactic was successful, by how much and at what cost, thereby allowing the fine tuning of resources to achieve a predetermined level of service quality.

(3) Linking pay and performance to quality

Once the measures and targets are well established and accepted by staff they can be linked to performance-related pay. BAA, through their well-established and sophisticated quality measurement systems, have linked service quality performance to the pay of their senior airport managers.

Five key measures of customer satisfaction are used to motivate managers to achieve their bonus which, in fact, is cut each year by 20 per cent for every satisfaction target missed. Not only by measuring service quality performance, but also by linking it to pay, service organisations can financially motivate their staff towards the achievement of target levels of customer satisfaction.

3.7 Quality measurement in different service environments

Whilst the preceding sections have described and discussed service quality measurement across all service organisations, some differences do exist between the different types of service. This section details some of the differences in service quality measurement between professional, mass and service shop organisations. Table 3.4 contains a summary of the main points.

Professional service organisations

In professional service organisations such as solicitors or consultancy companies, the long-term relationship between individual members of staff and individual customers is of vital importance. The complete satisfaction of each customer is important to ensure a continuing flow of work in the future. The specification of the service and the setting of quality expectations and targets are usually negotiated in advance with every customer and checked at the end of each job to ensure complete customer satisfaction. The nature of all jobs is checked to ensure that the organisation is capable of achieving the desired result. The other main form of quality control is of the inputs to the organisation, usually people. Staff selection, training, motivation and rewarding are activities crucial to professional organisations to ensure that they are not only technically competent but will be able to use the discretion available to them to ensure a high quality service for each client.

Quality tends to be measured internally by the use of formal quality audits and staff appraisals, and externally through the unstructured questioning of customers. Any dissatisfaction is dealt with and action taken, if necessary, for each individual customer.

Mass service organisations

In mass service organisations, for example BAA plc, the service relationship is not usually between individual members of staff and

Table 3.4: Key differences between service quality measurement in professional, mass and service shop organisations

	PROFESSIONAL	SERVICE SHOP	MASS
Service Relationship	long-term relationship between customer and staff important	←——————→	relationship between organisation and customer
Quality Specification	unique to job and negotiated with individual customer	←——————→	standardised service, requires setting of clear expectations
Key Resource For Control	staff	←——————→	facilities and staff
Control Systems			
internal systems	usually unstructured and informal	←——————→	structured and formal
customer satisfaction measurement	undertaken for every customer unstructured and informal	←——————→	customers sampled structured and formal mechanisms
Dissatisfaction	dealt with for each customer	←——————→	may lead to changes in design

individual customers, but is between the customer and the organisation as a whole. With less direct responsibility for quality and less discretion in the front line, many more structured quality control systems are required than for professional service organisations. Not only are controls of the inputs to the operations, both people and equipment, likely to be in place, but control of the process of service delivery and the results of service delivery are also likely to be measured. The difficulty here is that the organisation is serving a large number of customers on a frequent basis, and therefore has a wide range of customer expectations to meet. As a provider of standardised services, however, the image of the company and the setting of very clear customer expectations through the media or through advertising, is essential to try to ensure some degree of homogeneity of expectations. Formal systems might include frequent and well-structured surveys of customers to assess overall satisfaction levels, to monitor service delivery over time and to provide the case for future expenditure programmes. This will be offset by regular internal inspection procedures using either managers or mystery shoppers. As mass service industries tend to be capital-intensive, the provision of facilities is an important part of the service. Frequent internal assessment of the performance levels of equipment therefore, tend to be an important feature of quality control systems in such organisations. Again, similar to the softer people-based assessment of quality, the assessment of the quality of facilities is undertaken by asking customers to provide information about how satisfied they were with the facilities themselves. Any complaints or dissatisfaction expressed by individual customers, whilst acknowledged by the organisation, do not necessarily lead to remedial action. It is more likely that service design will be affected by longer term trends in satisfaction or dissatisfaction. Thus mass service organisations need to ensure that they have not only formal systems to measure the sources of dissatisfaction but also systems to track all the determinants, or characteristics, of service quality.

Service shops

Service shops are likely to fall between professional and mass service organisations. In this area the relationship between the individual service provider and the customer assumes more importance than it would in mass services, but less than in professional services. Service shops, however, do tend to use more service sampling than either professional or mass services. Unlike professional organisations, the service provided by service shops is more routine and therefore more easily sampled. As it is less standardised than mass services, however, the delivery of service is less formalised and therefore limited discretion and judgement may be used by staff. Even so, there are frequent interactions between staff and customers. This being the case, mystery shoppers or incognito managers assessing the delivery of service tend to be more common than in professional or mass service organisations.

3.8 Conclusion

Whilst service organisations acknowledge that service quality, its improvement and control are vital to competitive success and stability, many organisations, faced with the problems of intangibility and heterogeneity, find difficulty in creating robust and appropriate quality measurement systems. Quality can be measured over a range of twelve service factors. In this chapter mechanisms for their measurement have been described and the differences between the measurement of service quality performance in mass, service shop and professional service organisations identified.

3.9 Key points

- Providing a high level of service quality may be a source of competitive advantage.

- Achieving high service quality means ensuring all the factors of the service package meet customer requirements.

- There are twelve factors of service quality; reliability, responsiveness, aesthetics/appearance, cleanliness/tidiness, comfort, friendliness, communication, courtesy, competence, access, availability and security.

- The relative importance of the factors will vary from company to company and between customers.

- Service quality can be measured using external customer satisfaction measures and internal organisational quality systems at different stages of the service process.

- Both internal and external measures of the service quality factors are required to facilitate target setting, the tracking of the costs of changing quality targets and the linking of pay to quality performance.

- Quality control systems vary between professional, service shop and mass service organisations.

References

1 Carlzon J., *Moments of Truth*, Ballinger, 1987

2 Johnston R., 'A framework for developing a quality strategy in a customer processing operation', *International Journal of Quality and Reliability Management*, Vol. 4, No. 4, 1987, pp. 37-46

3 Parasuraman A., Zeithaml, V.A. and Berry, L.L., 'A Conceptual Model of Service Quality and its Implications For Future Research', *Journal of Marketing*, Vol. 49, No. 4, 1985, pp. 41-50

4 Johnston R., Fitzgerald L., Silvestro R. and Voss C., 'The determinants of service quality', in the proceedings of the First International Research Seminar in Service Management, Aix-en-Provence, 1990

4
Measuring Flexibility

'Flexibility is fashionable . . . More flexibility . . . , it is held, means more ability to move with customer needs, respond to competitive pressures and be closer to the market . . . Yet for all its new found popularity . . . the very word flexibility is used by different managers to mean different things.'

Slack, N. 'The Flexibility of Manufacturing Systems', *International Journal of Operations and Production Management*, vol. 7, no. 4, 1987

4.1 Introduction

Service flexibility is the ability of the service process to adapt to change. Flexibility is a concept which has been much explored in the manufacturing literature, particularly with the advent of flexible manufacturing systems, CAD/CAM and Just-in-Time, all of which are designed to enhance specific types of operational flexibility. Relatively little has been written specifically about flexibility in services. This is perhaps surprising, since the provision of service systems which can quickly adapt to meet the changing needs and expectations of customers is just as much a concern for the service manager as it is for managers in a manufacturing operation. Moreover, flexibility can be a major source of competitive differentiation for many services and a key order-winning criterion [1]. Exhibits 4.1, 4.2 and 4.3 below describe three organisations, a professional, service shop and mass service, and their respective challenges in providing flexible service to their customers.

Exhibit 4.1 Andersen Consulting

The management consulting arm of Andersen's is a professional service organisation which provides a highly customised service for a relatively low number of customers. It competes on the quality of its service and is frequently the highest bidder when a contract is put to tender. Andersen Consulting provides specialist consultancy in a wide variety of projects and applications. Each customer's problem is unique and demands a tailor-made solution. Specification of the contract is the first stage in every project and includes negotiation of the delivery date as well as the project definition. Projects can take days or months to complete, and scheduling jobs so that the delivery requirements of each customer are met and the right skill mix of staff assigned to each project, can be complex. It is not uncommon for customers to alter their project deadlines while work is in progress, necessitating unexpected changes to the work schedule.

Key challenges:

- *project specification flexibility*: every customer's requirements unique

- *delivery speed flexibility*: need to meet widely differing customer requirements in terms of project turnaround

Exhibit 4.2 Customer Enquiries Service

This service shop provides an enquiries service for the customers of a major utility. The service handles all telephone and written enquiries relating to invoices, field service repair and maintenance arrangements. The organisation believes that its enquiries service has a significant impact on customer perceptions of the whole organisation since it is, in effect, the company's front office. It considers that the provision of good quality and flexible service by its Enquiries Service can be a source of competitive advantage.

Most enquiries involve accessing customer account data from a centralised computer network. Staff are also trained in telephone answering procedures which are standardised throughout the organisation. All staff must attend a lengthy training course with the ultimate aim of solving queries during the first call.

Historical experience provides a fairly good indication of demand levels. There is considerable variation in the volume of calls received at different times of day and periods of the month. So the challenge for this organisation is to ensure that every customer is answered promptly on the first call, regardless of the volume of demand at any one time.

Key challenge:

- *volume flexibility*: the service has to be able to respond to widely varying levels of demand for any given period

Exhibit 4.3 British Rail

British Rail is a mass service which has a monopoly of rail travel, although it competes with other modes of transport. The service is segmented into first and second class travel to meet different passenger needs, but both services are highly standardised. Contact staff are among the less skilled in the organisation, the most skilled staff occupying management and engineering back office functions.

The organisation has adopted a highly complex matrix structure with business sectors, on the one hand, taking responsibility for revenue generation and regional production departments, on the other, responsible for cost centres. The business sectors and regional production managers agree annual contracts defining the level of service to be delivered by production management at an agreed cost to be met by the businesses.

The key challenge for British Rail is to design a timetable which satisfies large volumes of customers with differing requirements in terms of journey departure and arrival points, journey times and frequency. Once the timetable is set and disseminated to the public, it cannot be changed for six months. The timetable is therefore dependent upon demand forecasts: if forecasts overestimate demand then costly resources are under-utilised; if demand is underestimated trains are crowded and customers dissatisfied. Furthermore the journey times built into the timetable will rest on certain assumptions about the condition of the track and other plant and equipment. If a stretch of track is, in fact, in significantly worse condition than was predicted during the design of the timetable, trains will travel more slowly and journey times for the whole of the six-month period will be longer than specified in the timetable.

Key challenges:

- *travel specification flexibility*: customers have widely differing needs in terms of journey departure and arrival points, and frequency. The organisation cannot tailor journeys to suit individual needs in the short-term; the challenge is to build flexibility into the system in the long-term with a view to maximising customer satisfaction

- *delivery speed flexibility*: the ability to respond to different customer needs in terms of departure, arrival and travel times.

4.2   Different types of service flexibility

From the companies described in Exhibits 4.1, 4.2 and 4.3 we can see that there seem to be three different types of service flexibility: volume, delivery speed and specification flexibility. In the case of Andersen Consulting meeting widely differing customer requirements in terms of project completion times is a key challenge (delivery speed flexibility). In the Customer Enquiries Service the number of telephone calls received can vary at different times of day and year, and the challenge is to be able to respond flexibly to the different levels of demand without wasting resources in terms of staff time (volume flexibility). In British Rail the organisation cannot provide an individually customised service but needs to build long-term system flexibility into the journey timetable (specification flexibility).

Figure 4.1 summarises the definitions of each type of flexibility and illustrates the link with the ultimate objective of providing service flexibility, namely, that of generating customer satisfaction. Each of these is discussed below, together with the special problems which arise in the provision of flexibility because of the presence of the customer in the service process. The discussions draw upon the organisations described in Exhibits 4.1, 4.2 and 4.3.

Volume flexibility

Volume flexibility in services means the ability of the service process to respond to varying levels of demand. Services are primarily customer processing operations [2], and therefore the definition of volume will depend upon the nature of the business. In a retail shop, for example, it is likely to be defined in terms of the number of customers served; in a bank, in terms of the number of transactions processed; in an hotel, in terms of the numbers of rooms occupied.

The fact that the volume of services is dependent on the entry of the customer into the service system poses special problems for the service manager, particularly when customer demand is difficult to predict. Moreover, manufacturing strategies for meeting variable or cyclical demand by holding stock for future consumption are inapplicable in many services, since the production of the service and its consumption by the customer are often simultaneous. Service offerings such as rooms in an hotel, or seats on an airline, are instantly perishable; each time they are unused the sale is lost for ever. The provision of a service that can adapt to changes in demand without incurring high wastage is a considerable challenge for service managers.

Volume flexibility is a particular concern for the Customer Enquiries Service (Exhibit 4.2). Although customer demand is fairly predictable, peaking at certain hours and during certain times of the year, there is still considerable demand variability. If capacity in terms of the manning of telephones is set to meet peak levels of demand on a permanent basis, utilisation per staff member will be low. The challenge for the manager of this service is to be sufficiently flexible to meet peak demand without being wasteful of costly staff resources.

Figure 4.1: Summary of each type of flexibility

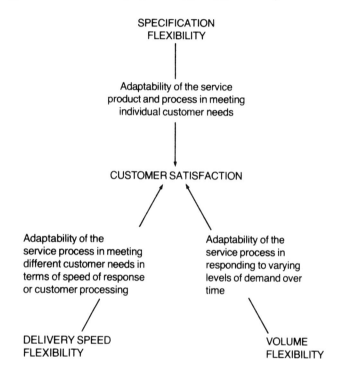

Delivery speed flexibility

Delivery in services tends to have a wider meaning than in manufacturing. In services such as transport, education and health care, there is not always a product or good to deliver. Delivery of service in these cases means responding to customers rather than delivering goods to them. Thus delivery speed in a customer enquiries service will have to do with the speed of telephone answering and the total time taken to process an enquiry. In a retail outlet it may be a matter of minimising queueing time. It should also be noted that the delivery speed required by customers will vary between services and will not necessarily mean *fast* speed but, rather, whatever speed is appropriate to meet customer needs. In a high-class restaurant, for example, the customer does not expect to be sped through the service process; on the contrary, the freedom to linger over the meal is something the customer is paying for.

Delivery speed can be measured both in terms of the time taken to respond to a customer's request for service and the time taken by the customer to pass through the service process. The provision of *flexible* delivery speed therefore means the ability to adapt the service process to meet different customer requirements in terms of either:

(1) appropriate *speed of response* to a request for service or for the delivery of goods; or

(2) appropriate *speed of customer processing*, that is, throughput time per customer

In Andersen Consulting (Exhibit 4.1), delivery flexibility means the ability to accommodate the project completion deadlines specified by customers; indeed project deadlines are not infrequently changed by customers whilst the project is in progress. In the Customer Enquiries Service (Exhibit 4.2) the customer seeks fast telephone response times. In British Rail (Exhibit 4.3), delivery flexibility is defined in terms of the ability to adapt journey speed and departure times. Whilst a certain degree of delivery flexibility may be built into the journey timetable with the provision of, for example, high speed non-stop journeys as well as local services, once the timetable is implemented there is little or no room for accommodating special customer needs.

In services, volume and delivery flexibility cannot be achieved as easily as in manufacturing since the production and consumption of services is often simultaneous. Failure to respond flexibly to changes in volume therefore usually has a direct effect upon delivery flexibility. If the number of customers using a service increases dramatically, there is likely to be less slack in the system to accommodate the delivery requirements of the next customer. Conversely, when capacity exceeds the volume of demand it is likely that the service will be more flexible in the lead and throughput times it can offer its customers. In the case of a car repair garage, if few repairs have been scheduled on a given day it is likely that a wide range of customer requirements in terms of completion time can be met. When the schedule is almost full, it is more likely that the customer will have to accept a delivery time specified by the garage attendant and that there will be little room to accommodate special requirements.

Again, the visibility of the service process to the customer makes delivery flexibility particularly difficult to provide because the amount of time spent with one customer can affect the waiting time of other customers and cause feelings of injustice, frustration and neglect.

Specification flexibility

Specification flexibility is the degree to which the service process can be adapted to meet individual customer needs (customisation). Service specification carries a wider meaning than product specification in manufacturing. Service specifications include not only that of the products and goods provided by the service, but also specification of the service process, the service environment and the precise nature of the interface between the service and the customer. When customer needs vary widely and there is a high degree of customisation, the matching of individual customer needs with the technical and interpersonal skills of staff may be an important element in the service specification. For example, in a nursing ward part of the provision of flexible service will be the matching of appropriate nurses to patients on the basis of their skills and patient needs.

As with the other types of flexibility, the problems associated with specification flexibility in services are compounded by the usual presence of the customer in the service process, which makes the success or failure of the organisation in responding to different customer needs highly visible. The use of advertising and other signals to inform the customer, before entering the service system, often plays an important part in ensuring that the customer's perception of the organisation's flexibility meets his or her expectation. It also ensures that the customer plays an appropriate role in the service system. If, for example, a customer enters a fast food service without understanding the standardised nature of the procedures and products available, he or she may well disrupt the service delivery process, thus inconveniencing other customers and reducing service flexibility in terms of response time. The onus is upon the service organisation to ensure that the customer is appropriately educated to use the service system[3].

Since the level of customisation is one of the dimensions used to classify services into the three generic types, professional services, by definition, offer the greatest specification flexibility, with mass services providing the least. This is manifest in the three organisations outlined in Exhibits 4.1, 4.2 and 4.3. In the management consultancy the service process begins with the individual specification of the project tailored to each customer's specific need. In the transport company the journey timetable cannot be adapted to meet individual customer needs. The infrastructure provides a wide variety of services and facilities but these are all standardised, not customised for individual passengers. The Customer Enquiries Service is mid-way between the two extremes, being considerably more standardised than the management consultancy yet handling a wide range of individual customer enquiries and therefore providing greater specification flexibility than is found in the transport company.

4.3 Measurement of flexibility

It is argued in Chapter 6 that innovation is difficult to measure directly. Similarly it is difficult to obtain direct measures of service flexibility. Exhibits 4.4, 4.5 and 4.6 describe the extent to which Andersen Consulting, the customer enquiries service of a utility and British Rail provide service flexibility and, where it is provided, the operational methods and techniques adopted. The performance indicators used to monitor service flexibility are also described.

Exhibit 4.4 Andersen Consulting

Andersen Consulting is a flat organisation with only four levels of consultant ranging from senior manager to staff grades. This structure helps to maximise flexibility in allocating staff to projects.

Capacity is defined almost exclusively in terms of labour hours and most front office activities tend to take place in the customer's premises. Labour hours are categorised as chargeable (to a customer) and non-chargeable. Non-chargeable hours include annual leave, supervision time and time spent on recruitment and training. Whilst the higher the proportion of chargeable hours the greater the revenue, it is recognised that a certain proportion of non-chargeable hours is essential if quality standards are to be maintained. The chargeable ratio for each grade of staff is targeted annually and closely monitored. Manipulation of non-chargeable hours can be used to match supply and demand, by increasing the proportion of chargeable hours during peak periods and scheduling non-chargeable time during periods of low demand.

Job scheduling is highly flexible and revised on a continuous basis. An administrator is responsible for assigning consultants to projects and building-in a certain level of non-chargeable hours. Project managers specify the skills required for a given job and will often request that a particular consultant be assigned to the work.

Operational flexibility is supported by the cross-training and multiskilling of staff to facilitate the matching of staff to projects. The skill mix of staff in terms of subject specialism and grade is monitored continuously in the light of new customer proposals which signal any medium-term changes in customer requirements.

When one of the offices has insufficient staff to meet the requirements of a particular project, staff from offices all over the world can be transferred to that location on a short-term contract basis to support the project. This is made possible because of the highly standardised nature of the training undergone by all consultants internationally. If it is not possible to allocate staff from elsewhere the project proposal is withdrawn. Eighty per cent of the company's business is repeat business, so only projects which can be adequately resourced so as to ensure delivery of a high quality service are accepted. Quality failure would only jeopardise future income streams.

The performance indicators below are regularly reported within the organisation and are believed to provide an indication of the business' success in providing service flexibility:

Performance Indicator	*Relevance to the provision of flexibility*
Job proposal acceptance rate *% repeat orders*	Indicate customer satisfaction with specification and delivery speed flexibility
Staff skill mix *% time spent on staff training*	The more skilled and versatile the staff the greater the flexibility in allocating staff to jobs to meet customer deadlines
Level of overtime worked	Indicates volume changes to which the company is responding

Exhibit 4.5 Customer Enquiries Service

The Enquiries Service has adopted a number of mechanisms to facilitate volume flexibility. Service opening hours have been increased in order to smooth demand and part-time staff are used to increase capacity at peak hours. The service has a fairly flat organisation structure, employing full- and part-time staff graded on the basis of experience and seniority. This facilitates the flexible allocation of staff to tasks. Furthermore, staff are trained to handle both telephone and written enquiries so that when there is an unpredicted increase in the number of telephone calls, the service unit manager can instruct staff working on written enquiries to transfer to telephone enquiries. This means that capacity for handling telephone calls can be increased by up to 60 per cent in a matter of minutes.

An electronic telephone system provides the service manager with minute-by-minute data on the number of calls answered, average length of telephone call per staff member, the number of unsuccessful (that is unanswered) calls, the average number of telephone rings before answering and so on. This enables him to decide how to allocate his staff between written and telephone enquiries, as well as monitor their individual performance. Targets are set in each of these areas and performance against them is monitored on a monthly basis by the operations director to whom the enquiries service manager reports. The performance indicators which have a bearing upon the provision of service flexibility are listed below:

Performance Indicator	*Relevance to the provision of flexibility*
% full to part time staff *Absenteeism*	Volume flexibility
Length of time callers had to wait for connection *% rejected calls* *No. minutes per day lines fully occupied* *% overtime to basic hours*	Ability of service to respond to changes in volume of demand. Also indicate delivery speed flexibility
Average length of telephone call *No. days taken to process written enquiries*	Delivery speed flexibility
Satisfaction with telephone answering response times	Customer satisfaction with delivery speed flexibility

Exhibit 4.6 British Rail

The core of the service contract is the journey timetable which is immensely complex and requires a lead time of fourteen months to produce. It is developed annually and revised after six months. Given the time taken to prepare the timetable there could be a lag of up to two years between the preparation of demand forecasts specifying passenger needs in terms of stopping points, journey frequency, length and start times, and the time of implementation.

Capacity in this organisation is defined primarily in terms of number of seats per vehicle. Given that it is not technically possible without significant extra resources to change the number of vehicles in the short term (this is specified in the annual service contract), the strategy is to attract passengers to travel during the periods of low demand by the use of pricing and promotion. Crowding of vehicles at peak hours is a problem for the organisation and a source of considerable dissatisfaction among passengers, so seat reservation systems have been strengthened.

The complexity of the service system allows little room for short- or medium-term flexibility in terms of volume, delivery speed or specification flexibility. Because the train timetable is dependent upon assumptions about track conditions which may prove to be inaccurate, some slack is built into each journey hour to allow for increased or decreased journey speed. The organisation also monitors passenger perceptions regularly to determine their expectations and evaluations of service. These are used as an input into the service and timetable design, thus supporting the provision of service flexibility in the long term.

Performance Indicator	*Relevance to the provision of flexibility*
Satisfaction with journey times and frequency *Satisfaction with train punctuality* *Satisfaction with seat availability in trains and crowding levels*	Customer satisfaction with specification and delivery speed flexibility
Train availability *Train punctuality* *Crowding levels*	Internal targets set to check to the service specification: results used as an input into timetable design. Relevant to all types of flexibility

Because of the difficulty in measuring flexibility directly, it tends to be either the determinants or the results of achieving flexibility that are measured rather than flexibility itself. The determinants are those aspects of the operation which contribute to its flexibility. In the consultancy (Exhibit 4.4), cross-training is central to the provision of volume flexibility, in that it facilitates job rotation and the international transferability of staff between offices. The number of training days and training expenditure per staff member are therefore closely monitored. In the Customer Enquiries Service (Exhibit 4.5), for example, a mix of full- and part-time staff is used in order to achieve volume flexibility; the proportion of part-time to full-time staff is therefore used as an indicator of service flexibility.

The results of providing, or of failing to provide, flexibility can also be measured. Qualitative data drawn from customers can be used to give an indication of how flexible the operation is perceived to be. A customer's reasons for not going ahead with a contract or project are analysed in the management consultancy, in order to identify the number of contracts lost due to failure to meet the customer's specification or delivery requirements. An increase in lost proposals might suggest that the service was failing to respond to changing customer needs either in terms of specification or delivery flexibility.

Just as service quality can be measured both quantitatively (hard measures) and qualitatively (soft measures), so can flexibility be measured by means of qualitative and perceptual as well as hard data. Qualitative data are likely to be particularly applicable to the measurement of specification flexibility. Similarly, internal measures and external or customer-based measures can be used. Table 4.1 provides illustrative examples of the performance indicators which service managers have been observed to use in order to measure service flexibility. Many of these measures are surrogate indicators of service flexibility rather than direct measures. For example, customer waiting time is not a direct measure of flexibility; nevertheless, lengthening of average waiting times can be indicative of a failure to provide volume flexibility. Whether or not a particular surrogate measure is an appropriate indicator of flexibility will depend upon the nature of flexibility in the particular service organisation.

In the next section the potential trade-offs between flexibility and the other determinants of performance are discussed. The implications of such trade-offs are that if flexibility is crucial to the service organisation's competitive success, then performance measurement systems which focus heavily on performance determinants which conflict with flexibility

Table 4.1: Examples of performance indicators for the measurement of service flexibility

TYPE OF FLEXIBILITY	PERFORMANCE INDICATORS
VOLUME	Number of customers/orders lost due to failure to meet demand % service availability Mix of staff availability (% part-timers, casual staff etc) Customer satisfaction with levels of crowding in the service environment
DELIVERY SPEED	% hours per day allocated for rush jobs (i.e. amount of slack in the schedule) % service facilities (e.g. beds in hospital ward) allocated for emergencies Speed of response Customer/enquiry/job throughput time Customer waiting time Frequency of service (e.g. train journey) % late deliveries Number of orders lost due to late delivery Customer satisfaction with delivery speed and responsiveness
SPECIFICATION	Number of different products and services delivered Skill mix of staff Number of days training per staff member per period Level of investment in staff training and recruitment Number of customers/orders lost due to failure to accommodate specification Customer satisfaction with the adaptability of the service in meeting special requirements Customer satisfaction with range of products and services

are likely to be dysfunctional. It has been argued in Chapter 1 that a range of performance measures are needed to monitor the performance of a service business and that, in particular, measures should be in place to monitor those aspects which are crucial to competitive success. Consequently, if a business is competing on flexibility, it is important to implement measures of performance against this criterion, despite the fact that performance in this dimension can be difficult to measure.

4.4 Trade-offs between flexibility and the other performance criteria

Flexibility can form a powerful source of competitive advantage, providing a means of differentiating one's services from those of one's competitors. Moreover, because it is often difficult to offer flexibility it can form a barrier to new entrants into the market and further strengthen competitive position. The logistics of providing flexibility have to be considered at the service design stage; indeed, if flexibility is identified as a means of competitive differentiation, its provision will be a design parameter. When designing a type of flexibility into a service it is important to realise its potential trade-offs with the other performance determinants, particularly resource utilisation.

The full costs and benefits of providing flexibility are not always fully appreciated at the design stage. Take, for example, the introduction of ATMs in the banks. These facilities dramatically increased the volume and delivery flexibility of banking services, providing 24-hour availability and fast throughput times. When they were introduced, however, few of the banks realised the impact this would have on the nature of the service interface between the bank and its customers. The frequency of contact between service staff and customers dropped so much that opportunities for cross-selling other products and services were dramatically reduced. It took some time before the banks started to address the need to find new ways of developing the retail side of their business.

Flexibility can conflict with cost objectives and resource utilisation. A highly trained and multi-skilled staff may facilitate the provision of a wider range of services (specification flexibility) and will improve flexibility in responding to variable demand (volume flexibility) by increasing the mobility of staff between functions; but high salary levels and heavy recruitment and training costs are incurred. A company which has adopted a differentiation strategy may well accept increased labour costs because it is believed that the customer will be prepared to pay a premium for service flexibility. A company which is competing on cost, on the other hand, may decide to trade-off a certain degree of operational flexibility in order to minimise cost and thus pass on reduced prices to the customer. Similarly, increasing service availability by extending opening hours or increasing the number of service outlets – and thus providing volume flexibility – will be costly in terms of labour and capital resources and may mean low utilisation. These costs have to be balanced against the potential advantages of maximising potential revenues and of possibly locking the customer into the service.

There can also be trade-offs not only between flexibility and the other performance criteria, but also the different types of flexibility. A retailer may, for example, have high stock levels of a particular product in order to meet the peaks in variable demand (volume flexibility), but this may constrain flexibility in altering the mix of products and services (specification flexibility) and thus reduce market responsiveness.

Decisions about which type of flexibility should be designed into the service have to be made in the light of customer needs and the service organisation's competitive positioning. Prior recognition of the costs and benefits involved in the provision of a particular type of flexibility is central to the development of a service design which enables the organisation to compete effectively in the market.

4.5 Flexibility in different service types

The arguments for the provision of flexibility differ between the three generic service types: professional, service shop and mass services. Each of these services may attempt to provide one or a combination of the different types of service flexibility to suit its competitive strategy. The differences between the three service types lie in the scope for providing the different types of flexibility and the mechanisms used to achieve them.

Volume flexibility

In terms of staff numbers, professional services tend not to change their capacity in the short-term because of the high cost of recruitment and training. Nevertheless, these services tend to have greater short-term flexibility than do mass services. Flexible job scheduling systems are used to support the negotiation of delivery dates with customers, whilst knowledge of customer proposals and current work in progress facilitate short and medium-term capacity planning. Given the high skill levels of contact staff, multi-skilling and cross-training are commonly used to maximise flexibility in assigning staff to jobs. This also enables staff to be transferred between functions, between front and back office activities or even between service units, in order to meet unpredictable peak demands. Flat organisation structures also tend to be a feature of professional services, again in order to maximise flexibility in assigning staff to jobs.

Mass services, on the other hand, are usually hierarchical and highly functionalised organisations. The service systems are large and complex and therefore cannot respond quickly to changes in short-term demand. Incremental changes in capacity tend to be greater in mass services: whilst in professional services capacity may be increased in the medium-term by adding a new member of staff, in a mass service a step change in capacity is likely to mean a considerably larger investment, such as the addition of capital equipment or new buildings. Decisions to change capacity in mass services tend, therefore, to be long-term, and level capacity strategies are adopted. Systems are often designed around peak times and there is more reliance on pricing strategies and seasonal promotions to smooth demand. Since the skill levels of contact staff tend to be lower than in the professional services, labour flexibility is achieved less by means of multi-skilling and job rotation than by the use of part-timers and floating staff to cover peak demand, and by the use of casual staff to meet seasonal demand.

In service shops there is less short-term flexibility than in a professional service, but the time horizons of capacity planning strategies tend to be shorter than for mass services. A mix of the mechanisms for achieving flexibility used by professional and mass services is adopted.

Delivery speed flexibility

In the case of professional companies, delivery lead times vary from job to job and are often negotiated with individual customers. These services also need to be highly flexible in the time made available to customers, according to their widely varying needs. In a mass service, where delivery lead and throughput times tend to be more highly standardised, the aim is not so much flexible throughput times but rather optimising throughput speed. In a service shop there is less variability in throughput time than in a professional service but staff have more discretion over the amount of time they spend with individual customers than in a mass service.

Specification flexibility

Since one of the dimensions which distinguish professional services, service shops and mass services is the level of customisation (see Chapter 1), professional services, by definition, offer greater specification flexibility than do mass services. In a professional service, specification of the service is likely to take place within the service process. In the case of a consultation with a general practitioner, management consultant or lawyer, for example, the service process begins with the customer's specification of his or her enquiry. In standardised services the provision of specification flexibility tends to be a matter of providing a *range* of options from which the customer can choose, rather than enabling the individual customer to participate in the development of the specification itself. In mass services, therefore, specification takes place before the customer enters the service process and the customer has little opportunity to participate in the service specification during the process. Service shops are positioned mid-way along this continuum. Whilst the customer cannot participate in the process of service specification to the extent that is possible in a professional service, service shops tend to have to deal with a wider range of customer requirements than do mass services, thus reducing opportunities for standardisation.

Table 4.2 overleaf summarises the differences between professional and mass services in terms of the scope for providing service flexibility. Table 4.3 lists a number of different mechanisms which can be used to support operational flexibility and indicates the extent to which each mechanism is likely to be used in each of the three service types.

To summarise, it is suggested in Figure 4.2 that the different types of flexibility correlate with the volume of customers per period.

4.6 Conclusion

The presence of the customer in the service process creates special problems for service managers attempting to provide specification, delivery speed or volume flexibility. Because it is difficult to provide, flexibility can, however, be a powerful source of competitive differentiation which can form a barrier to entry for competitors. Developing appropriate measures of flexibility is also a major challenge, but necessary for those companies competing on service flexibility. In professional services there tends to be more scope for providing short-term flexibility than in service shops and mass services, where adapting to different customer needs may mean step changes in service design and capital investment which can only be made in the medium to long term.

Table 4.2: Scope for the provision of service flexibility in professional and mass organisations

TYPE OF FLEXIBILITY	PROFESSIONAL SERVICE	MASS SERVICE
VOLUME	High degree of short term flexibility.	Little short term flexibility. Use of level capacity strategies.
DELIVERY SPEED	Flexibility in response and throughput times by manipulating job schedule. Staff discretion over time spent per customer.	Little flexibility. Average response and throughput times built into the system. Variations reduce system efficiency.
SPECIFICATION	High degree of flexibility. Matching of customer to service process on an individual basis.	Little short term flexibility. Flexibility may be built into the service system design in the long term.

NB Service shops are positioned midway between these two extremes.

*Table 4.3: The extent to which each mechanism for supporting
operational flexibility is used in different service types*

MECHANISM	PROFESSIONAL	SERVICE SHOP	MASS
Job Scheduling	High ←――――――――――――→ Low		
Negotiation of Delivery Dates with Customer	High ←――――――――――――→ Low		
Reservation and Appointment Systems	Very widespread ←――――――――――→ Less often		
Queueing Systems	Less often ←――――――――→ Widespread		
Job Rotation and Staff Transfer	High ←――――――――――――→ Low		
Cross-training and Multiskilling	High ←――――――――――――→ Low		
Part-time and Floating Staff	Low ←――――――――――――→ High		
Spreading service Availability (e.g. Extending Hours, ATMS)	Low ←――――――――――――→ High		
Pricing and Promotion Strategies to Smooth Demand	Low ←――――――――――――→ High		

Figure. 4.2: The relationship between types of flexibility and volume of customers per period

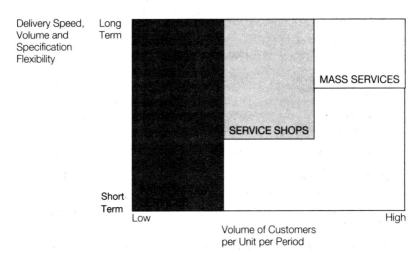

4.7 Key points

- Flexibility can be a key source of competitive differentiation.

- There are three types of operational flexibility: volume flexibility, specification flexibility and delivery speed flexibility.

- Like innovation, flexibility is difficult to measure directly; rather it tends to be the determinants or results of achieving flexibility that are measured rather than flexibility itself. Measures can be hard or soft, internal or external.

- Given the possible trade-offs between flexibility and the other performance criteria, decisions as to which types of flexibility should be designed into the service are strategic decisions to be made in the light of customer needs and the organisation's competitive positioning.

- Scope for short-term flexibility varies from very little in mass services to a great deal in professional services. All services have some scope for providing volume, specification and delivery speed flexibility in the long-term.

- The mechanisms used to support the provision of flexible service vary between the three service types. Principal mechanisms used by professional services include job scheduling, reservation systems, job rotation and cross-training; those used by mass services include queueing systems, part-time staff, extending opening hours, and pricing and promotion to smooth demand.

References

1 Hill T., *Manufacturing Strategy – The Strategic Management of the Manufacturing Function*, Macmillan, 1985

2 Johnston R., 'A Framework for Developing a Quality Strategy in a Customer Processing Operation', *International Journal of Quality and Reliability Management*, Vol. 4, No. 4, 1987, pp 35-44

3 Johnston R., 'The Customer as Employee', *International Journal of Operations and Production Management*, Vol. 9, No. 5, 1989

Further reading

Bartezzaghi E. and Turco F., 'The Impact of Just-in-Time on Production System Performance: An Analytical Framework', *International Journal of Operations and Production Management*, Vol. 9, No. 8, 1989

Slack N., 'Flexibility as a Manufacturing Objective', *International Journal of Operations and Production Management*, Vol. 3, No. 3, 1983

5
Measurement of Resource Utilisation

'Given infinite resources any system, however badly managed, might perform satisfactorily in respect of customer service. The problem . . . stems from the fact that operating systems must satisfy multiple objectives. Customer service must be provided simultaneously with the achievement of effective or efficient . . . utilisation of resources',

Wild R., *Concepts for Operations Management*, John Wiley, 1977

5.1 Introduction

Resource utilisation is a performance criterion which evaluates how efficiently resources are utilised in the delivery of services; or taking a slightly different angle, how productive the organisation is in providing its services, given the level of capital and other resources. The implications of utilising resources efficiently are clear. If a service organisation can provide the same level of service with fewer resources than its competitors, this will enable it either to operate on higher profit margins or to reduce its price with a view to increasing market share.

5.2 The use of budgets to control resource utilisation

Budgets represent the overall plan for making the best possible use of the human, physical and financial resources of an organisation. Budgets are normally tied to a particular time period and set in advance of that period; they are part of the feedforward control process outlined in Chapter 1. Typically the budget will include quantities of resources, costs and revenues for a projected activity level, the activity level normally being defined as the planned number of services sold. Implicit in the formulation of the budget are assumptions relating the quantity and cost of inputs to the quantity and cost of outputs. The relationship between budgeted input and output levels can be represented using the input-process-output model introduced in Chapter 1. This is shown in Figure 5.1, page 83, in which money units are shown at the top, and physical units at the bottom of the diagram.

One purpose of setting a budget is to provide a plan for managers to work towards and a yardstick against which actual performance can be measured. Differences between actual results and the budget can arise from changes either in the level of activity (that is the services sold), or the cost and quantity of resources used to produce the sales. The cause of the difference, or variance, has implications for management control and the corrective action required. Changes in the level of sales need to be reported to the marketing department. Such changes are essentially planning variances caused by changes in market share or market size. The technique for identifying this variance is to remove the effects of the change in sales volume by producing a revised or flexed budget. Differences between the flexed budget and actual results are termed control variances which have resulted from the use of more or less resources and/or payment of higher or lower prices for those resources than planned.

Many organisations design their budgeting systems so that actual quantities of resources, costs and revenues can be compared with previous years' results in addition to comparison with the current year's budget.

This chapter focuses on the relationship between input, process and output, and the measures used by organisations to monitor these relationships. These results can be used to make comparisons over time, to budget and between SBUs.

5.3 Measurement of resource utilisation

In manufacturing, resource utilisation is often measured in terms of productivity, that is, a ratio of inputs to outputs:

$$\text{Productivity} = \frac{\text{Outputs}}{\text{Inputs}}$$

Improving productivity can thus be achieved either by reducing the level of inputs, increasing the level of outputs, or both. Similarly, resource utilisation in services can also be measured as a ratio of inputs to outputs. The definition of resource utilisation in services is, however, broader than that of productivity in manufacturing since not all services are, in a straightforward sense, in the business of transforming inputs into outputs. Some services are performances[1], for example, spectator sports and entertainment, lectures, physiotherapy and child-minding. Other services provide facilities for the use of customers, for example, hotels, leisure centres and airports.

Figure 5.1 indicates the different types of measures of input and output which can be used in service organisations and suggests that input and output measures fall into two different categories:

(1) those itemised in the top half of the diagram, which evaluate inputs and outputs in monetary terms;

(2) those itemised in the bottom half, which measure inputs and outputs in terms of units.

Unlike most manufacturing processes customers participate in many services, thus forming inputs and outputs to the process. A major issue for service industries is the difficulty of measuring outputs and of tracing service inputs to those outputs. The next section explores those difficulties.

Measurement of service outputs

Since many services do not operate a straightforward transformation process, units of service output can be difficult to quantify. Whilst in manufacturing companies outputs are defined as the products or goods produced, in service companies outputs often take other forms. Service outputs can be measured in terms of the number of customers who have passed through the service process, the number of services or goods delivered or sold, or, paradoxically perhaps, in terms of the number of resources consumed. For example, an hotel may use the number of occupied rooms as an output measure. A management consultancy may use the number of hours chargeable to clients as an output measure, comparing this with the total number of available man-hours as the input measure.

Service outputs can also be evaluated in monetary terms. The three principal measures are: revenue generated from service delivery, profit and added value. Added value is defined as revenue less the cost of materials and services purchased from outside the organisation (as opposed to those manufactured or processed by the organisation itself).

The difficulty of quantifying service outputs is enhanced by the intangibility of many service offerings. Even in the case of services which do provide some tangible outputs, these are usually not the only items provided by that service. The tangible outputs of a restaurant are the food and drink, but this is not all the customer is paying for; his or her purchase also involves having the food served in a particular way and in a certain type of environment. The intangibility of services thus makes the quantification of outputs difficult.

The heterogeneity of services also causes problems in measuring outputs. In a manufacturing company the product is likely to be homogeneous (the classic 'can of beans'). Counting the number of units produced is therefore relatively straightforward and can provide a meaningful indication of the level of production output.

By contrast, the number of services delivered by a service organisation can provide little indication of how much service or how many services have been provided. A service unit may provide a wide range of services each day, every one taking various amounts of time and requiring a different combination of resources and expertise. A general practitioner, for example, will typically serve a range of patients with widely varying needs and expectations. Because the needs and treatment of each patient are different it is difficult to compare the number of consultations on different days, or the number of consultations per practitioner or per service unit.

Measurement of service inputs

Inputs into the service process include the resources used to provide the service, not only labour, but material, plant and equipment; in service organisations the participating customers also form inputs into the service process. In order to decide which input measure to use, service managers need to assess which are the most significant inputs. For example, in labour intensive businesses, such as professional services, where labour represents a high proportion of the total resources used, labour may be the most appropriate input measure. Labour can be measured in terms of cost or in terms of the units of labour used, such as number of man days or hours. Other resources may be measured in terms of units of time or numbers of resources used. For instance, in order to measure the utilisation of an ATM in a bank, the number of machine hours available may be a useful input measure; British Rail use the number of train miles provided as an input measure. Alternatively the inputs to the service could be measured in terms of cost, both of people and other resources.

In Chapter 2 the notion of cost traceability was discussed, our contention being that it varied with the volume of customers per business unit per period. Where the volume of customers is low and service provision is mainly people-based, labour hours, which represent the major share of total costs, can often be traced to each individual job or customer. Where volume is high and service is provided by means of a complex combination of both labour and capital equipment, there tends to be a greater proportion of allocated costs and the input costs of providing each individual service can be difficult to trace. This has obvious implications for the differences between professional services, service shops and mass services, since these are dimensions which distinguish the three service types. Mass services are more capital intensive and return on investment may be here an appropriate measure of resource utilisation.

The problem of tracing the costs of inputs to outputs is further complicated by the heterogeneity of service processes and the simultaneity of service production and consumption. It can be hard to determine how much of each resource has been used in providing each service and hence the costs incurred by each. In some services customers' needs differ so much that there is considerable variety in the time spent with each one, the staff skill mix and other resources required to service each customer. Each customer may purchase a different combination of products and services or follow a different route through the service process, so that tracing the cost of serving each customer can be complex, time-consuming and expensive.

The fact that it is difficult to measure resource utilisation does not, however, lessen its importance as a performance criterion. Service organisations may choose to use one or more input/output ratios as part of their range of business performance measures. Any one of the input indicators featured in Figure 5.1 can be juxtaposed against any of the output measures depending on the organisation's cost structure and the ·nature of the inputs and outputs to the service process. Figures 5.2 to 5.6 below provide instances of the combination of input/output measures actually used by a number of service organisations.

Figure 5.2 provides examples of services which measure labour utilisation using a ratio of units of human resource consumed to labour hours available. In Barclays Bank units of resource consumed are measured in terms of the number of transactions processed; in Andersen Consulting the number of consultant hours charged to the client is used; while in the Customer Enquiries Service the amount of time actually spent answering the telephone is used to measure inputs consumed.

Figure 5.3 provides examples of utilisation of other resources, such as equipment and facilities, by comparing units of resources consumed with those available. Commonwealth Hotels measure the number of rooms occupied as a proportion of hotel rooms available; theatres measure the number of seats occupied during a performance as a proportion of total seats available; British Rail measure the number of passenger miles travelled compared with the number of train miles available.

Figures 5.4 and 5.5 provide instances of companies which use numbers of customers as their output measure. The number of customers is compared with numbers of staff or labour hours to provide customer: staff ratios (Figure 5.4) and with total cost to provide cost per customer ratios

(Figure 5.5). Figure 5.6 juxtaposes the number of customers to total revenue in order to measure revenue per customer.

All the resource utilisation measures described in Figures 5.2 to 5.6 were routinely reported within the budgeting system. Comparisons were made between actual results and budget and between input and output levels. In addition some companies made comparisons between actual results of different SBUs. This information was often published as a league table of results.

Exhibits 5.1, 5.2 and 5.3 describe a professional service, a service shop and a mass service, and outline the resource utilisation issues which arise in these organisations, the varying levels of cost traceability in each and the resource utilisation measures used.

Exhibit 5.1 A firm of auditors

This professional service is one of the large UK-based auditing firms. Established over a century ago, it now has offices in twenty towns and cities and employs about 3000 staff. In common with all the other large auditing firms, it offers a range of specialised services including auditing, taxation advice, management consultancy, business investigations, insolvency, trust administration and technical training. It employs specialised staff in each area. The company considers itself to be differentiating on the basis of its efficient, personal and friendly service. All clients' enquiries are directed through a partner who becomes the account holder and always deals personally with that client. Audits represent the bulk of business, so there is a relatively stable client base and considerable customer loyalty. Most new clients come by recommendation from other clients, bank managers or solicitors. The organisation structure is flat with only five main grades of staff. Capacity is defined mainly in terms of man hours. A senior partner comments: 'We are quite hard pressed at times, but we don't turn away work. Expansion is measured by the number of people, not by turnover. The budgets are related to the number of people that we can usefully employ. Turnover expands with people.'

Scheduling and the allocation of staff to jobs is the responsibility of an administrator in each office. The schedule is altered on a daily basis as new jobs are received, and often clients amend their deadlines. Demand is highly seasonal, most companies requiring audits for their December or March year-ends. Job lengths vary considerably from one man day to, say, 3,000 man hours.

Figure 5.1: Input – Process – Output model

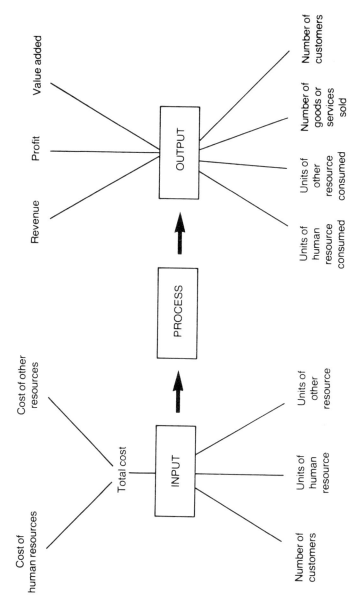

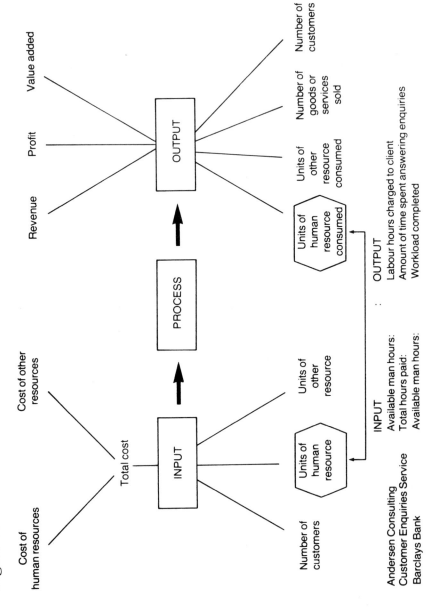

Figure 5.2: Labour utilisation

Figure 5.3: Utilisation of other resources

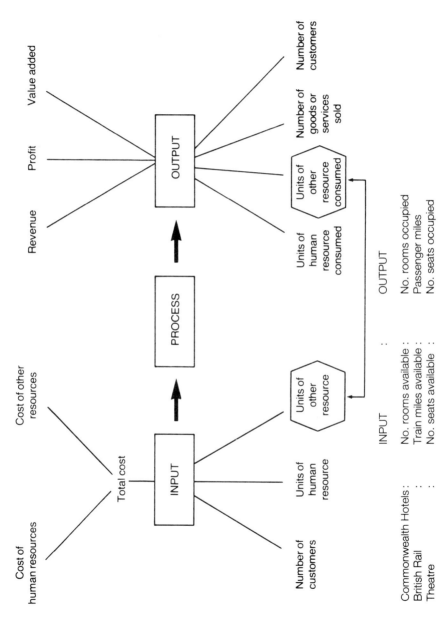

Figure 5.4: Customer : staff ratio

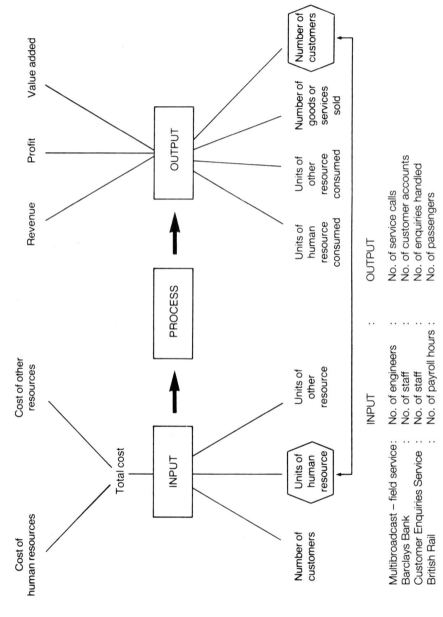

INPUT	:		OUTPUT
Multibroadcast – field service:	No. of engineers	:	No. of service calls
Barclays Bank	No. of staff	:	No. of customer accounts
Customer Enquiries Service	No. of staff	:	No. of enquiries handled
British Rail	No. of payroll hours	:	No. of passengers

Figure 5.5: Cost per customer ratio

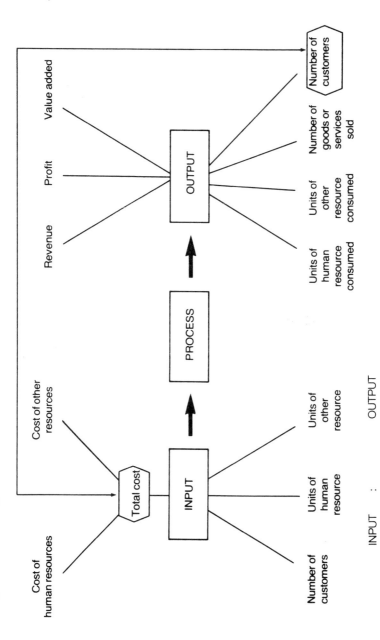

Figure 5.6: Revenue per customer ratio

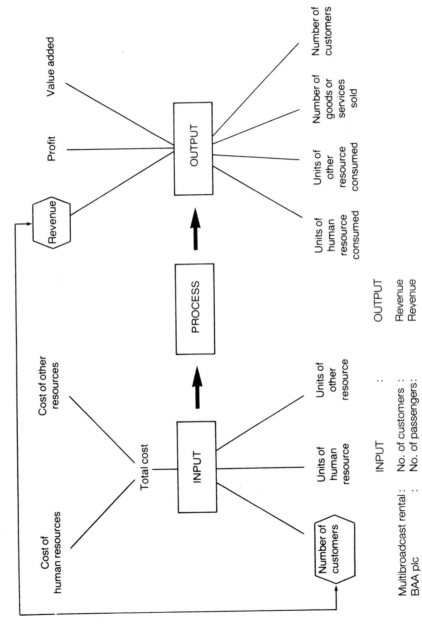

Everyone in the organisation, except administrators, completes time sheets. These show how many hours each person has spent on which job, and how many hours have been spent on non-chargeable activities such as supervision, recruitment and training. This means that, because staff represent the vast majority of the costs, costs are largely traceable to individual jobs and only a small proportion of the costs are allocated. The time sheets are used to price each job and to calculate the chargeable ratio (percentage of non-chargeable to chargeable time), which is the organisation's key measure of resource utilisation (see Figure 5.7, overleaf). Variances between the actual time taken to do a job, and hence its cost, and the estimate on which the quotation was based are also reported on a monthly basis, together with the profit figure.

Exhibit 5.2 Barclays Bank plc

Barclays, one of the five major UK high street banks, services both personal customers and corporate accounts. Its range of products and services exceeds 350 and Barclays nowadays competes in many areas not traditionally associated with banking, such as mortgages and insurance. In this service shop capacity is defined primarily in terms of staff numbers, although the introduction of Automatic Teller Machines (ATMs) is making the service interface increasingly equipment-based.

There are three sources of bank revenue: interest charged on loans to customers, interest on loans to the Bank of England (generated from customer credit accounts) and commission charges. Gross margins per product are known since they are related to lending and borrowing from the Bank of England. Interest charges and interest payments to customers are generally tied to bank base rates. Branch costs comprise 60 per cent staff costs, 14 per cent premises and equipment costs and 26 per cent other costs. No attempt is made to trace any of these costs to products. The costing system is illustrated in Figure 2.3, page 25.

Quarterly reports to regional offices compare actual with budgeted costs. Every six months a 'league table' of branches is circulated within each region indicating the resource utilisation of each branch in terms of a ratio of average debit and credit balances per head of staff. Barclays also use a branch productivity index which is reported to regional offices on a monthly basis. The productivity index is a ratio of measured workload to available man-hours (see Figure 5.8). Every branch records on a monthly basis the number of clerical transactions processed, including the number of letters sent, the number of cheques and direct debit payments processed, and so on. This information is entered on to a computer

Figure 5.7: Professional service: A firm of auditors

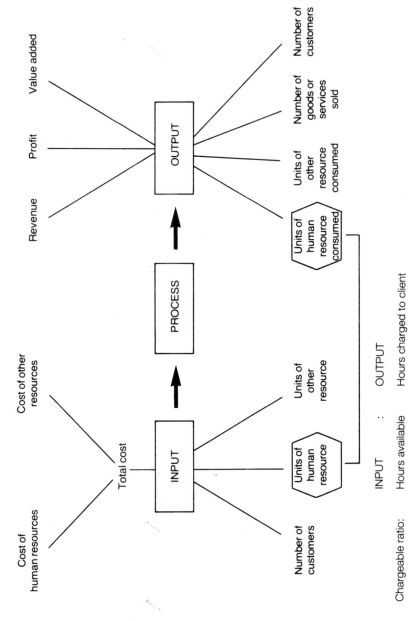

Figure 5.8: Service shop: Barclays Bank plc

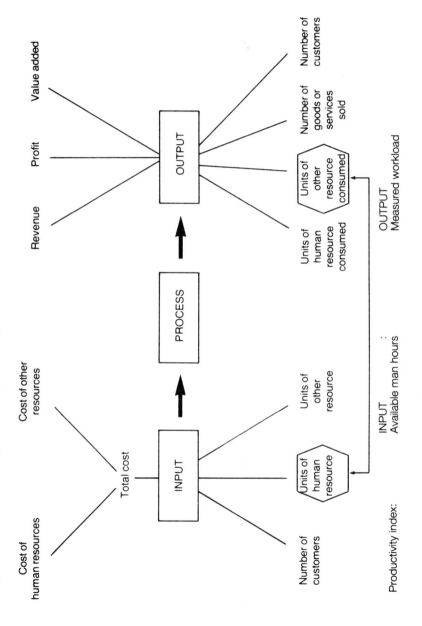

together with the number of man hours worked and a productivity ratio is obtained. The ratio is reported to regional offices which use the information both as a measure of branch performance and to support staffing decisions. The recruitment and appointment of staff to branch positions are regional rather than branch decisions.

Branches are targeted to achieve standard levels of productivity on the basis of branch size. If a branch achieves a considerably higher level of productivity than is standard (that is, a higher workload than is normally achieved given the number of man hours available) it is assumed that service levels are likely to be deteriorating and additional staff are allocated to the branch. There can, however, be a lag of up to four months between the initially observed high productivity ratio and the decision to increase staff numbers. Conversely, if the productivity index is consistently below standard, staff levels in the branch are decreased. The three- or four-month time lag is caused by the fact that regional offices tend to be reluctant to allocate additional staff to a branch which may only be experiencing a temporary increase in workload. A 'float' of staff is available within each region to meet short-term staff shortages. Nevertheless, some branch staff have expressed the view that this system is too slow in responding to the resourcing needs of branches.

The bank considers itself to be competing on service quality. It is noticeable, however, that whilst branch productivity is closely monitored by regional offices, there are no formal quality measures in place to offset these measures. There is, therefore, no way of knowing to what extent quality levels suffer when branch productivity exceeds the standard. The bank is, however, aware of this gap in their control information systems and is currently in the process of redressing this situation.

Exhibit 5.3 BAA plc

BAA plc is a mass service which owns and operates seven of the UK's airports including its largest sites, Heathrow and Gatwick. Its business is the provision of landing space for aircraft and waiting areas for airline passengers. It generates its revenues from two principal sources:

(a) *Airlines*: the airlines pay landing fees based upon frequency of their touchdowns and take-offs, time of use, cargo tonnage and numbers of passengers carried; *and*

(b) *Concessionaires*: the shops, catering and other commercial outlets in the airports which have concessions with the airport terminal, usually based upon a percentage of sales revenues.

BAA has comparatively little control over passenger perceptions of the service levels delivered in the airports because many of the services offered there are the responsibility of other organisations. For instance, the Civil Aviation Authority is responsible for air traffic control and, in collaboration with the airlines, for flight scheduling; the manning of ticket and check-in desks is the responsibility of the airlines; and Government authorities are responsible for passport and immigration control. The quality of service in the car parks, shops and catering outlets are, of course, the responsibility of the concessionaires.

Furthermore the vast majority of staff whom passengers meet during their passage through the airports are not employed by BAA but by these other organisations. Most passengers who complain about airport services are oblivious of the fact that the transport terminal's direct responsibility for service is in fact limited to the following main areas:

- airport design and layout;
- provision of equipment such as escalators, lifts, travelators, and baggage reclaim units;
- cleanliness and condition of airport;
- provision of luggage trolleys for passenger use;
- porterage;
- sign-posting in the airport;
- airport security;
- provision of flight information systems and information desks.

Capacity planning in the airports is a long-term process. Ultimately capacity is determined by the size of the airports, the number of termini within an airport, the number of runways within the terminal and the size of the passenger waiting areas. These cannot be changed in the short-term. Airport design is based upon forecasts of demand; usually airport size will be determined by the demand level which is anticipated when the airport has saturated its local market. Typically it will take around twenty years before an airport reaches this 'mature' phase in its life cycle.

In the medium-term capacity within an airport terminal is determined by the number of check-in desks made available to the airlines and the number of passenger facilities such as luggage trolleys. There is a clear trade-off here between flexibility in meeting variable demand and in the maximisation of resource utilisation in terms of passengers per terminal. If the facilities provided are such that demand can be met at all peak periods, then the resources are likely to be under-utilised during most of the year, and, in the case of the trolleys, passenger waiting areas would appear cluttered most of the time. The airport terminal operation therefore designs its service facilities so as to meet demand at all times except during exceptional peaks.

Cost traceability is difficult in this organisation. In fact, all airport costs are allocated to the two revenue centres, the airlines and concessionaires. Exactly which and how many of the airports' resources and facilities are used to provide service to the two revenue centres is unknown. Moreover, costs can neither be traced to passengers, passenger types, individual flights or airlines. The airport terminals use a number of measures of resource utilisation which are reported within the termini and to head office on a monthly basis:

- total costs per passenger;
- passengers per pay-roll hour;
- passengers per unit of employee cost;
- revenue per employee.

These are illustrated in Figure 5.9. Monthly reports compare costs to both budgeted and previous year equivalents and airport managers are required to provide written explanations of any major variances.

BAA is very much aware that one of the easiest ways of improving performance against these utilisation ratios is by cutting costs and reducing service levels. These utilisation measures are therefore counterbalanced with a range of quality measures, both internal and external (these are discussed in Chapter 3, Table 3.2). The organisation is keen to demonstrate to its customers that its financial returns are not being generated at the expense of quality. Both the resource utilisation and quality indicators for each terminal are therefore reported in the annual report and accounts. Moreover the quality targets are tied to the management bonus system to deter managers from achieving short-term profit at the expense of service quality (the bonus system is described in Chapter 7, Exhibit 7.1).

5.4 Potential trade-offs with resource utilisation

The maximisation of resource utilisation may involve trade-offs with the other performance determinants: innovation, flexibility and quality. The decision as to what levels should be targeted for each of the performance determinants will depend upon the service organisation's competitive

Figure 5.9: Mass service: BAA plc

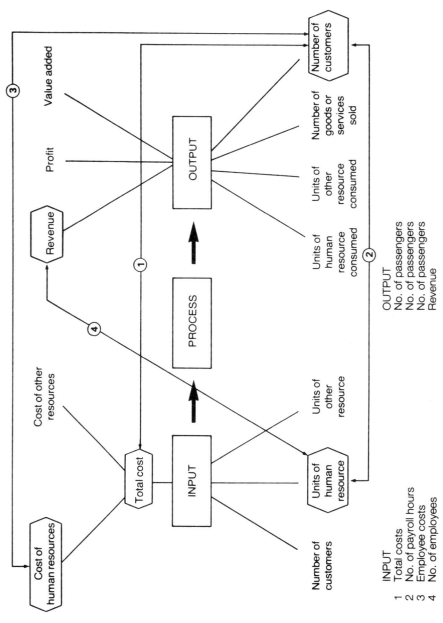

INPUT
1 Total costs
2 No. of payroll hours
3 Employee costs
4 No. of employees

OUTPUT
No. of passengers
No. of passengers
No. of passengers
Revenue

strategy. A company which is competing on cost is likely to focus on resource utilisation because cost reduction relative to the volume of services delivered is a major source of competitive advantage. A service which has adopted a strategy of differentiation on the basis of service quality, on the other hand, may be prepared to accept lower resource utilisation in order to ensure high levels of service quality.

It is important that the potential trade-offs with resource utilisation are clearly understood at the service design stage and that the performance measurement systems are designed accordingly, with appropriate emphasis on the different performance criteria. Thus, if a company is competing on service quality, it may be dysfunctional to focus staff attention too closely on resource utilisation ratios, even though it may be desirable to take such measures. In particular it may be inappropriate to target the performance of individual staff on the basis of utilisation measures. If, for instance, bank cashiers are pressurised into processing a certain number of transactions a day, this may have a negative impact upon their treatment of customers and could result in a deterioration of service quality.

It is arguable that, whether or not a service organisation considers itself to be a cost leader or a differentiator, quality measures should be in place to offset the utilisation measures, since there is a danger that some managers may seek to maximise utilisation at the expense of quality, particularly if their personal performance is measured on this basis. BAA (described in Exhibit 5.3) recognises that the easiest way to improve utilisation is to cut service levels; that is, to reduce the level of cost per passenger. It therefore considers it to be vital to use measures of both resource utilisation and of service quality, in order to ensure that managers are not achieving high utilisation at the expense of quality, or vice versa.

A company which competes on innovation may also have to forego the optimisation of resource utilisation. Introducing new products and services may mean, for example, having to spend more time on training activities and supervision; this will in turn reduce the amount of time staff spend on activities which are directly chargeable to customers. Furthermore, when bringing a new service on stream initial 'teething' problems are likely to reduce operational efficiency, and the implementation of effective control systems may take time. Launching new services is inherently risky; but a focus on the maximisation of resource utilisation can often lead to risk aversion. Again the relative weight which should be afforded to these two potentially conflicting performance criteria is a strategic decision.

There can be trade-offs between resource utilisation and each of the three types of service flexibility:

(1) Volume flexibility

Designing a system which can respond to a wide variety of demand levels often means low utilisation during slumps in demand. In Barclays Bank (described in Exhibit 5.2) volume flexibility is provided partly by means of ATM facilities. The more ATMs are installed in a branch the more flexible the system will be in responding to different demand levels; conversely, the fewer the number of machines, the higher the utilisation rate of each ATM.

(2) Delivery speed flexibility

Flexible scheduling is often achieved by allowing slack in the schedule so that rush jobs, emergencies or jobs for 'premium' or regular customers can be fitted in. Examples of services which might adopt such tactics might be car repair garages, hospital wards or translation services. This strategy, however, runs the inherent risk of low utilisation if no such jobs materialise.

(3) Specification flexibility

Standardisation of the service process is often a good way of ensuring maximum utilisation but this means reducing customisation and specification flexibility.

5.5 Resource utilisation issues in the different service types

One of the characteristics mentioned in Chapter 1 which distinguish the three generic types of service is that professional services tend to be people-based, whilst mass services tend to be more equipment-based, and service shops are positioned between these two extremes. This means that in a professional service, capacity will be largely defined in terms of labour hours. In the other two services, capacity will be determined by a complex mix of human and non-human resources. In professional services, therefore, resource utilisation ratios are likely to use staff headcount, units of staff time, or labour costs as the input measure. Service shops and mass services may need to consider the utilisation of the full range of resources used to provide the service. Although these organisations may use utilisation ratios with labour input measures, they are likely to supplement these with ratios which include input measures of other resources such as capital, or total cost.

The varying levels of cost traceability also have implications for the measurement of resource utilisation in the three service types, traceability being high in professional firms, medium in service shops and low in mass services. Because of the high proportion of labour costs in professional firms, the input costs are largely represented by labour hours per service. Labour hours are generally relatively easy to trace to individual jobs since the job scheduling systems provide information on the amount of time each staff member spends on a job. Diary systems are often used whereby each member of staff keeps a record of the amount of time spent on each project or activity. The firm of auditors described in Exhibit 5.1 is an example of a company where labour represents by far the largest proportion of costs. Labour hours are easily traced to individual members of staff and charged to clients according to staff grades. The main measure of resource utilisation in this firm is therefore the ratio of chargeable hours to non-chargeable hours (hours spent on activities such as recruitment, training and so on).

In mass services, which tend to be more equipment-based than professional services, the proportion of capital costs is much higher and costs tend to be allocated to services. The large volume of jobs which are processed per service unit per day also makes it more difficult and costly to obtain precise information as to the level of resources consumed in the delivery of each service. In BAA (Exhibit 5.3), for example, all terminal costs are allocated to the two revenue centres (the fee paying airlines and the concessionaires). The actual costs cannot even be traced to the two revenue centres, let alone a lower level of aggregation such as individual flights or passengers. The resource utilisation measures used in this organisation are a ratio of total costs to passengers, passengers per pay-roll hour and passengers per unit of employee cost.

In service shops there is often an understanding of gross margins, with direct costs being traced to individual products and services. However, unlike professional services, in service shops direct costs tend to exclude labour hours which are treated as overheads, even though labour represents a significant proportion of total costs. As a result, the traceability of costs in these organisations is more difficult than in professional firms, but gross margins per product and service tend to be understood; in mass services such as BAA even gross profits per product or service are often unknown. Exhibit 5.2 describes a typical service shop. In Barclays Bank interest charges and interest payments to customers are typically tied to bank base rates; gross margins per service are therefore known because they are related to Barclays' lending to and borrowing from the central bank. However, even though staff represent

60 per cent of total branch costs, no attempt is made to trace these or indeed any other branch overheads to products. The main productivity indicator, given the high proportion of staff costs, is a ratio of measured workload to available man hours, reported monthly. Branches are targeted to achieve particular levels of productivity on the basis of branch size; the indicator is used both to measure branch performance and to support staff resourcing decisions taken at regional level. Barclays also use a ratio of average debit and credit balances per head of staff as a measure of branch resource utilisation, although this is reported less frequently.

5.6 Conclusion

Measuring resource utilisation in service organisations is difficult because of the heterogeneity of services, the simultaneity of production and consumption and the complexity, particularly in mass services, of tracing inputs to outputs. Nevertheless, a wide variety of input and output measures can be used to generate utilisation ratios. The selection of appropriate measures will depend upon the type of service in question and its cost structure. The dysfunctional effects which can arise from an over-emphasis on resource utilisation can be overcome through the use of a balanced range of performance measures, including, in particular, measures of those performance determinants with which there is a direct trade-off.

5.7 Key points

- Efficient resource utilisation can be a key source of competitive advantage, enabling an organisation to operate on higher profit margins, or alternatively to pass on reduced prices to its customers.

- Resource utilisation in services can be more problematical to measure than in manufacturing because of the heterogeneity of many services and the simultaneity of their production and consumption.

- Planned resource utilisation levels are implicit in the formulation of budgets. Actual resource utilisation measures are often compared to both the budget and previous years' results.

- Over-emphasis on resource utilisation can, however, be potentially dysfunctional: the trade-offs which can exist between resource utilisation and the other determinants of performance, quality, innovation and flexibility, should be recognised in the setting of targets.

- Resource utilisation can be measured by means of a ratio of service inputs and outputs. These can be measured in terms of monetary value, numbers of units and numbers of customers

- In a professional service, labour is the key resource and utilisation measures are therefore likely to take the form of labour productivity indicators. Although service shops and mass services may also use ratios with labour input measures, they are likely to supplement these with ratios which include input measures of other resources or total cost.

- Cost traceability varies between the three service types, being high in professional services, medium in service shops and low in mass services.

References
[1] Berry L.L., Zeithaml V.A. and Parasuraman A., 'Quality Counts in Services, Too', *Business Horizons*, May-June 1985

Further reading
Blois K.J., 'Productivity and Effectiveness in Service Firms', *Service Industries Journal*, Vol. 4, No. 3, November 1984

Eilon S., 'Framework for Profitability and Productivity Measures', *Interfaces*, Vol. 15, No. 3, May/June 1985

Sink D. Scott, *Productivity Management: Planning, Measurement and Evaluation, Control and Improvement*, John Wiley, 1985

6
Measurement of Innovation

'Intense competition in technology and an economy that increasingly relies on services for expansion has made the successful development of new services a key to success for many firms'

de Bretani, U., 'Success and failure in new industrial services', *Journal of Product Innovation Management*, No 6, 1989, pp. 239-258

6.1 Introduction

The impact of innovation on company performance can be great, however, the amount of written material on the nature and measurement of innovation in the service sector is limited. Furthermore, we have not found many measures used by our case study companies of either the performance of individual innovations or of the processes that lead to successful innovations. This chapter therefore reflects the early stage of development of innovation definition and measurement in service businesses. Whilst we attempt to address measurement issues later in the chapter, the early sections explore the nature of innovation in service industries and the processes leading to innovation.

An innovation is an application of ideas and knowledge to meet a current or future market need. In service industries, innovation can be related to a product, a service or the process of service delivery. Innovation encompasses not only the successful development of completely new products and services, but also the smaller, incremental innovations that can modify and improve existing products, services and delivery systems.

Innovations can be front-office based, involving the development of new services, or back-office based, often using technology to improve productivity. An example of the former would be the use of portable personal computers to support the selling of financial services. An example of the latter is the development of software to automate the documentation processes in a freight forwarding company. Innovations in the back office can substantially increase productivity, but also, if managed well, may lead to customer benefits such as faster turn-round of enquiries and orders.

In some instances innovations will change the nature not only of a service but of the whole service system, and in some cases the whole of the industry. Exhibits 6.1 and 6.2 briefly describe the effects of two innovations in service industries.

Exhibit 6.1 Computers in the banking industry

'The new information technology based systems in banking . . . . extend beyond back office efficiency considerations into strategic marketing goals in creating new products and increased organisational flexibility to meet new needs and wants'[1].

Exhibit 6.2 Automatic stock exchange transactions

'Automation of [the stock exchange] securities trading process . . . . . changed the entire structure of that industry. Under the old paper-based systems, shares traded had to be physically delivered from the seller's agent to the buyer's. As daily volumes approached twelve million shares, only the big banks could hire and manage enough people to keep track of their securities trades each day. Smaller firms began to fail because they could neither control nor process securities in a timely fashion. Finally, Wall Street firms formed the Central Certificate Services which brought it all under one roof. After five or six years, the system became totally electronic and smaller brokers could tie into the depository. Today automated clearing houses handle virtually all private and Government transactions.'[2]

Quinn and *Gagnon*[2] describe a wide range of similar innovations that have had a significant impact on other service industries. Much of the change within an industry, however, will come about through smaller, incremental innovations. Although each one may be only small, the total effect can be large. Exhibit 6.3 describes a number of small but significant innovations made by a television rental company.

Exhibit 6.3 Innovation in television rental

Television rental is an industry that has ridden on a wave of technological innovation. During the early 1970s rental companies experienced high demand primarily due to the nature of the product; it was both expensive and had low reliability. As prices fell and reliability improved, rental companies maintained their position through the continued technical innovation of the products they provided; video recorders, flat, square screens, remote control and video-text. However, by the end of the 1980s, the steam had run out, at least temporarily, from the innovations in the products rented.

One response to this is illustrated by the rental company, Multibroadcast. In their bid to remain competitive in this static but competitive market, they have sought small innovations in their service delivery system to help them develop a distinctive and better quality service than their competitors. These innovations included the development of service centres away from the shops, in order to focus on efficient and high quality after-sales support. This new service organisation, now separated from sales, was given its own brand name, Multi-care. This further enabled the organisation to sell its product servicing to third parties such as Argos. Another innovation was the change of dress of the service engineer from an overall to a shirt and tie so that the customer would see him as a skilled technician rather than a mechanic. A series of small innovations such as these has led to a major change in the nature of the service offered.

In services, new ideas can often be implemented speedily, but this also means that they can readily be copied. In such an environment, the ability to continue the process of innovation may be crucial for leading edge companies. Exhibit 6.4 describes some of the new products and services introduced by Bob Payton in his efforts to stay ahead in his field.

Exhibit 6.4 Theme restaurants in the UK

In the late 1970s, Bob Payton introduced Chicago-style deep dish pizzas to the UK in the very innovative and highly successful 'Chicago Pizza Pie Factory'. In a comparatively short period of time other restaurants were copying the deep dish pizza, and often his American 'factory' restaurant approach. Today deep-dish pizzas can be eaten in most towns in the UK. Despite this rapid (and flattering) copying, Payton was able to sustain the growth of his restaurant chain through continued innovation. His subsequent innovations included spare rib restaurants (The Chicago Rib Shack) and applying his US style to fish and chips (Payton's Plaice!). He was also able to sustain his original deep-dish pizza concept by establishing a high quality of service that was difficult to copy.

6.2 The process of innovation

The process of innovation first of all involves bringing together knowledge of market needs with the technical means to develop a new idea, concept or invention. A new idea by itself is insufficient to guarantee a successful innovation. The idea, concept or invention has to be turned into an effective product or service which must be developed, debugged, tested and finally launched. This is the process of innovation which is illustrated in Figure 6.1, opposite.

Each step identified in Figure 6.1 requires simultaneous activities by marketing and market research, and by the service process/product development function in order to co-ordinate the technical means of provision and the development of the delivery system with the market need.

Despite the obvious need for an effective innovation process, it is often not in place in many companies. This point is illustrated in the following quote by the director of a major bank.

'The development of a new service is usually characterised by trial and error. Developers translate a subjective description of a need into an operational concept that may bear only a remote resemblance to the original ideal. No one systematically quantifies the process or devises tests to ensure that the service is complete, rational, and fulfils the original need objectively. No R & D departments, laboratories or service engineers define and oversee the design.' [3]

6.3 Difficulties in innovation

Despite its importance in many service companies, innovation is not as developed a function as it is in manufacturing. The main characteristics of services identified in Chapter 1, intangibility, simultaneity, heterogeneity and perishability, pose particular barriers to innovation and may explain to a certain extent why innovation is less developed in service companies.

Intangibility

Intangibility poses problems for both customers and management. Because services are often intangible and therefore invisible, customers cannot easily examine them prior to purchase. Thus potential purchasers of new services cannot compare them with alternative offerings unless they sample them. It is important, therefore, either that good marketing is used to inform customers of the difference between one company's offering and those of its competitors, or that more tangible signals are used, such as the packaging of the service, or visible clues provided in the service environment.

Figure 6.1: The process of service innovation

CONCEPT DEVELOPMENT AND ANALYSIS
↓
PROTOTYPE SERVICE DEVELOPMENT
↓
PROTOTYPE SERVICE TEST AND DEBUG
↓
FULL LAUNCH OF NEW SERVICE
↓
SERVICE IMPROVEMENT

A second difficulty arising from intangibility is that because services are processes and not physical entities, they may be more easy to modify than physical products and physical processes. Thus changes to the service offering may take place relatively quickly and easily and, indeed, such changes and developments may take place, initiated by individual service workers, without the knowledge of management or 'service designers' or without the appropriate organisational learning taking place. Such innovation may also be at the expense of customers and service quality.

A third difficulty arising from intangibility is that innovations may be more easily copied by competitors. Furthermore, because service innovations may not be patentable, such copying may not be preventable.

Simultaneity

The simultaneity of the production and consumption of many services means that services are instantly perishable and cannot be held in stock. Thus capacity planning and management of demand may be critical in service companies. Demand, also, can vary considerably and either has to be met immediately or lost. The impact of service innovation may therefore be hard to ascertain. Some organisations choose to introduce a new service at a time of low demand so that demand levels and the requisite resources may be more accurately assessed.

Heterogeneity

Because service tends to be produced and consumed simultaneously, and is created and consumed at the staff-customer interface, the service experience is likely to vary each and every time. Both staff and customers play roles in the delivery of the service and there is likely to be inherent variation in this process [4]. The degree of variation expected may well depend upon the degree of standardisation of the service and the amount of technology applied at the customer interface.

Furthermore, it may be argued that in service industries the process involving customer and server constantly undergoes innovation, and the participants in more customised operations undergo a learning process during the delivery of the service. Innovation may therefore be a naturally occurring phenomenon during service delivery.

An additional obstacle has been identified by *Scarborough* and *Lannon* [1] who consider that there may be difficulties in service industries in developing and implementing innovation. They believe that there may be problems in integrating innovations into the whole system as many service innovations are information-based and have ramifications for the company-wide information system.

6.4 *Measuring innovation*

We would suggest that service innovation can be measured in two ways. First, a company can measure the performance of the innovation itself, that is the results of its implementation. Second, a company should be aware of the determinants of success and failure in the process of service innovation and should therefore adopt measures to monitor that process.

Measuring the success of an innovation – the results

At its simplest, the ultimate test of the success of an innovation is its effect on a company's profits. However, because of the many other factors which affect a firm's profit figure, it is unlikely that such a measure would in itself provide adequate detailed information to enable a company to judge the level of success of the innovation or to help it develop better innovations in the future.

We would propose that the success or failure of an innovation, i.e., the outcome of the innovation process, can be measured along the other five dimensions discussed in Chapter 1; financial performance, competitiveness, quality, flexibility, and resource utilisation. Using this categorisation, companies may then review the success of an innovation by asking key questions about these dimensions and use measures described in the other chapters of this book. These dimensions and key questions are shown in Table 6.1.

Table 6.1: Dimensions for measuring the success of an innovation

FINANCIAL	Has the innovation improved financial performance?
COMPETITIVENESS	Has it made the company more competitive?
QUALITY	Has it improved quality?
FLEXIBILITY	Has the company's ability to be flexible improved?
RESOURCE UTILISATION	Has resource utilisation improved?

Many companies that gauge innovation success use a wide range of measures. A study by *de Bretani* [5] of practice in 115 service companies found that companies measured the success of their innovations in terms not only of financial performance but also of other performance criteria such as competitive performance and quality. The financial measures she identified included not only profitability but also the meeting of cost targets and the degree to which costs were lowered. Competitive performance measures included successfully meeting or exceeding market share objectives, sales objectives, growth, relative level of customer use and effect on the company reputation and image. Service quality measures included the levels of perceived service outcome and the customer service experience. A study by *Voss* [6] of innovations in freight forwarding companies and software houses identified additional measures of product and service reliability and improved delivery, e.g. speed or user-friendliness of the service. Additionally, some of the measures of success attempted to calculate the cross-impact of the innovation, for example whether or not it also boosted or reduced customer use of the company's other products and services. These measures of the results of service innovation are summarised in Table 6.2

Measuring the performance of the innovation process

Successful innovations depend on good planning. A number of studies have been conducted in order to identify the determinants of success and failure in the innovation process. Although most studies have been of products, there have been a number of studies of service innovations, notably *Voss* [6] and *de Bretani* [5].

Table 6.2: Examples of measures of the results of service innovation

FINANCIAL MEASURES

Achieving high overall profitability
Substantially lowering costs for the firm
Performing below expected costs
Achieving important cost efficiencies for the firm

COMPETITIVENESS MEASURES

Exceeding market share objectives
Exceeding sales/customer use level objectives
Exceeding sales/customer use growth objectives
Achieving high relative market share
Having a strong positive impact on company image/reputation
Giving the company an important competitive advantage
Enhanced sales/customer use of other products or services

QUALITY MEASURES

Resulting in service 'outcome' superior to competitors
Resulting in 'service experience' superior to competitors
Having unique benefits, perceived as superior to competitors
Greater reliability
More responsive
More user-friendly

Sources: Voss (1985), de Bretani (1989)

There were a number of common characteristics associated with successful innovation processes found in both studies. First, attention to the market; successful innovations were characterised by one or more of the following market-orientated factors: they satisfied clearly identified customer needs and wants; they expanded current markets or were aimed at high-growth markets; or they were consistent with existing customer values/operating systems.

Second, successful innovation was characterised by factors such as efficient development work, short development lead times, good communication among different functions during development, employee involvement, internal marketing of the concept of the new service, full testing before release and formal post-launch evaluation. There were also a number of organisational aspects, in particular, the existence of a champion for the new service, both at the development stage and at the marketing stage.

Third, both studies also found the strategies of the firms to be important to innovation success. They tended to be risk-takers and to have innovator (rather than follower) strategies. Successful innovations were consistent with these strategies. They were typically a core or primary service of the firm and fitted the marketing, market research, sales, promotional, financial, human resource capabilities and resources, as also existing service delivery systems and managerial skills and preferences. These findings are summarised in Table 6.3, overleaf.

We would propose that the process of developing service innovations can be measured along three dimensions: cost (how much does it *cost* to develop a new service?), *effectiveness* (how effective is the process of service innovation?) and *speed* (how fast can a new service be developed?).

Cost

There are a number of measures of cost. First, the cost of developing a new service and its breakdown between the above stages. Second, the percentage of turnover invested in developing new services, products and processes.

Effectiveness

The effectiveness of an innovation process is more difficult to measure. In practice we are asking how innovative the organisation is. A number of proxy measures can be used to measure innovativeness. For example, how many new services are developed per year? How does this compare with major competitors? What percentage of service concepts reach launch? Of those services that are launched, how many are successes, how many are failures?

Speed

This dimension is currently the subject of much attention in manufacturing, where Japanese pressure and 'time based competition' are leading to efforts to reduce product development lead times. This is bringing innovative new approaches such as 'simultaneous engineering'. Performance can be measured in terms of the lead time of the innovation process, and in terms of the time for each of the individual stages (see Figure 6.1). For example, the time from concept to prototype, or the time from prototype to launch could be measured. Speed can also be

Table 6.3: Determinants of success in the process of innovation

DETERMINANT	EXAMPLE
Attention to the Market	Satisfied clearly identified customer needs/wants Solved important client problems Responded to changes in customer needs and wants Expanded current markets Aimed at high-growth markets Consistent with customer values/operating systems
Development Process	Efficient development work Short development lead times Availability of resources Good communications internally among different functions Good communication outside the firm Employee involvement Marketed new service to own frontline personnel Fully tested before release Formal post-launch evaluation Project champion during innovation development Project champion during commercialisation
Strategic and Business Fit	Risk-taking strategy Innovator (rather than follower) strategy Fit with marketing research capabilities and resources Fit with sales and promotional capabilities and resources Core or primary service of firm Fit with financial resources of firm Fit with existing service delivery system Fit with expertise/human resource capability Fit with managerial skills and preferences Fit with back office facilities/processes

measured in terms of response time. Innovation can often be in response to customer request, environmental change, technology change or competitor action. An example of such a measure is how long it takes to respond to, and possibly copy, a competitor's innovation.

These measures of the process of service innovation are summarised in Table 6.4, overleaf.

6.5 Issues in service innovation

Innovation is a complex task to manage, and there are a number of issues facing service organisations.

Uncontrolled innovation can have negative effects. For example a leading bank introduced a large number of new financial products. Many of these were only moderately successful and after a while were withdrawn. However, since many financial products, such as endowment policies and insurance, have a long life, the bank was left to service a diverse set of low usage, low profit services from which it could not withdraw in the short term.

Some measures of performance can have a negative impact on innovation. In particular, measures of conformity to process specification may, on the one hand, lead to a high quality service process; on the other hand, they may deter managers from rethinking the process and improving it through innovation. If innovation is a high corporate priority, it can be argued that quality measures should be dynamic and reactive to changes in the market place and assist in identifying new and changing customer needs.

The cross-impact of an innovation can be both positive and negative. Such a case was the introduction of Automated Teller Machines in banking, which was successful in many ways. Most banks, however, failed to predict some of the negative impacts of reducing contact between the cashiers and the customers, notably, the significantly reduced ability of the banks to sell other financial services.

6.6 Innovation in different service environments

In most of the earlier chapters it has been argued that there are significant differences between different types of service organisations: professional services, service shops and mass services. Research in innovation is as yet at too early a stage to draw conclusions in this area. As a result, we do not feel it possible or valid to present conclusions for different types of service.

Table 6.4: Measures of the process of innovation

DIMENSION	EXAMPLE
COST	Average development cost per service
	Development cost of individual service
	% of turnover spent on developing new services, products and processes
EFFECTIVENESS	How many new services developed p.a.
	% new services that are successful
SPEED	Concept to service launch time
	Concept to prototype time
	Prototype to launch time
	Time to adopt new concept from outside the firm

6.7 Conclusion

Innovation is a critical activity for service companies, but it is both difficult to do well and to measure its performance. This chapter has argued that measurement of performance should focus on two areas, the performance of individual innovations (the outcome of the innovation process), and the innovation process itself. Individual innovations can be measured in terms of the dimensions of performance described in Table 6.2. In addition to developing a framework for measuring innovation performance, this chapter has described the determinants of innovation success summarised in Table 6.3. Finally, measures of the process of service innovation have been described and are summarised in Table 6.4.

6.8 Key points

● Innovation can have a major impact on company performance.

● An appropriate process is required for the development of innovations.

● Measurement of innovation should be both of the performance of the innovation itself and of the process of developing it.

● The measurement of the performance of an innovation should be in terms of its impact on competitiveness, quality, flexibility, financial performance and resource utilisation.

● The measurement of the process of innovation should be based upon the existence of a a well defined process; its cost, effectiveness and speed.

● The determinants of the success of an innovation are the attention to the market, the development process and its strategic and business fit.

References

1 Scarborough H. and Lannon R., 'The Management of Innovation in the Financial Services Sector: a Case Study', *Journal of Marketing Management*, Vol. 5, No. 1, 1989, pp. 51-62

2 Quinn J.B. and Gagnon C.E., 'Will Services Follow Manufacturing into Decline?', *Harvard Business Review*, Vol. 64, No. 6, November-December 1986, pp. 95-103

3 Shostack G.L., 'Designing Services that Deliver', *Harvard Business Review*, Vol. 62, No. 1, January-February 1984, pp. 133-139

4 Morris B. and Johnston R., 'Dealing with Inherent Variability – the Difference between Service and Manufacturing Explained', *International Journal of Operations and Production Management*, Vol. 7, No. 4, 1987, pp. 13-22

5 de Bretani U., 'Success and Failure in New Industrial Services', *Journal of Product Innovation Management* No. 6, 1989, pp. 239-258

6 Voss C.A., 'Determinants of Success in the Development of Applications Software', *Journal of Product Innovation Management*, No. 23, 1985, pp. 122-129

Performance Measures: Choice and Implementation

'The management accounting profession is . . . faced with the opportunity of integrating and co-ordinating the output of non-financial data emanating from corporate activities in . . . service industries, into management accounting systems. The relevance of considering qualitative and non-financial quantitative information encompassing the management of strategic and operational, organisational processes cannot be over-emphasised. Empirical evidence suggests a growing role for this type of information in enterprise management and management accountants cannot ignore calls for their involvement in this respect'.

Bromwich M. and Bhimani A., *Management Accounting: Evolution not Revolution*, CIMA, 1989

7.1 Introduction

In this final chapter we do three things. We begin by showing how managers may develop a balanced range of performance measures which match their company's *service type*, while also taking into account the *environment* in which they are competing and the *strategy* they have chosen to implement in the search for a sustainable competitive advantage. Second, we consider the choice of appropriate ways of motivating staff using incentive schemes linked to the performance measurement system. Finally, we consider some aspects of how to introduce and run an integrated performance measurement system.

7.2 Development of a range of performance measures

The managers of every service organisation will need to develop their own set of performance measures to help them devise a strategy to gain and retain a competitive advantage in the field in which they operate. We have proposed that the set should encompass measures, both results and determinants, across all six generic performance dimensions: competitiveness, financial, quality, flexibility, resource utilisation and innovation (see Figure 7.1, overleaf).

Figure 7.1: Dimensions of Performance

RESULTS:	COMPETITIVENESS FINANCIAL PERFORMANCE
DETERMINANTS:	QUALITY FLEXIBILITY RESOURCE UTILISATION INNOVATION

The performance measurement system will be determined by the competitive environment, business strategy and service type, see Figure 7.2. Each of these will be considered in turn in the development of a balanced range of performance measures.

Competitive environment

The *nature* of the performance measurement system will be a function of the environment in which the business is operating, for example, the size, the complexity and turbulence of the competitive arena. This decision will in turn determine whether the business needs to build an *interactive* system focusing on strategic threats and facilitating regular dialogue between top management and operating management, or can largely rely on delegated control of day-to-day operations, with reporting to top management on an *exception* basis to ensure sustained profitability.

Business strategy

The actual mix and weighting of the set of performance measures used – *what* will be measured – will be influenced by the business's chosen competitive strategy. Is the business a *cost leader*, a *differentiator*, or using either of these to focus on a narrow target market segment [1]? If the business is a cost leader, we would suggest that it should be emphasising tight cost control by focusing on measures of resource utilisation. If it is competing based on a strategy of differentiation through quality, say, then it should be focusing on measures of quality.

No matter what the type of strategy, when designing a performance measurement system it is important, firstly, to consider both the current and future competitive strategies. For instance, while technological innovation may not currently be on the horizon as a competitive weapon it could be strategically important for the future of the business and thus worthy of top management's regular scrutiny. Secondly, whilst quality is not an order-winning criterion[2] in every industry, in most of those where it is not order-winning it *is* an order-qualifying criterion, so it has to be measured.

While the strategic focus may change over time, we believe that organisations should adopt measures across ALL six dimensions, though their detail and sophistication will vary with strategic needs.

Figure 7.2: Factors which determine the performance measurement system

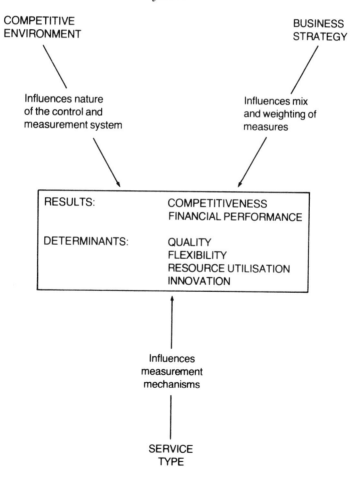

COMPETITIVE
ENVIRONMENT

BUSINESS
STRATEGY

Influences nature
of the control and
measurement system

Influences mix
and weighting of
measures

RESULTS: COMPETITIVENESS
             FINANCIAL PERFORMANCE

DETERMINANTS: QUALITY
               FLEXIBILITY
               RESOURCE UTILISATION
               INNOVATION

Influences
measurement
mechanisms

SERVICE
TYPE

Service type

Services can be classified as professional, service shop or mass using the classification scheme introduced in Chapter 1; their key characteristics are represented in Figure 7.3. Many companies will be a hybrid mix of two or more of the three archetypes, and any company may change its service type over time as a result of strategic choice. We believe that the performance measures and the measurement mechanisms used by service organisations vary to some extent between these three service types. In Chapter 2 it is argued that there are no significant differences in the way different types of service organisation measure competitiveness. The measurement of financial performance also tends not to vary by service type, although we have observed that the different cost structures of professional and mass services make costs more easily traceable in professional services. The analysis of the profitability of individual services and products tends to be more difficult in mass services due to the high proportion of allocated costs.

There appear to be more significant differences in the way professional and mass services measure quality, flexibility and resource utilisation. In Chapter 3 we highlighted the quality factors against which service organisations measure quality and suggested that whilst the factors which professional and mass services measure may not vary by service type, the measurement mechanisms *are* different. Whilst professional services can afford to measure quality during each stage of the service process, that is, the inputs, outputs and during service delivery, mass services tend to rely more heavily on the measurement of service outputs and sample-based surveys of customer satisfaction.

In Chapter 4, it is argued that measures of flexibility, which tend to be either satisfaction measures or measures of the factors which facilitate service flexibility, may also vary between professional and mass services, for both the scope for providing flexibility and the means by which it is provided varies between the service types. In Chapter 5, on the measurement of resource utilisation, we suggest that whilst professional services tend to focus on the utilisation of human resources, mass services are likely to supplement such measures with ratios involving other resources or total cost.

In Chapter 6 we distinguish between measures of the innovation process and measures of the service innovation itself. We have not observed much variation in the way professional and mass services measure the success of the innovation process, although we recognise that relatively little research has been carried out in this area to date. The performance

Figure 7.3: Service Classification Scheme

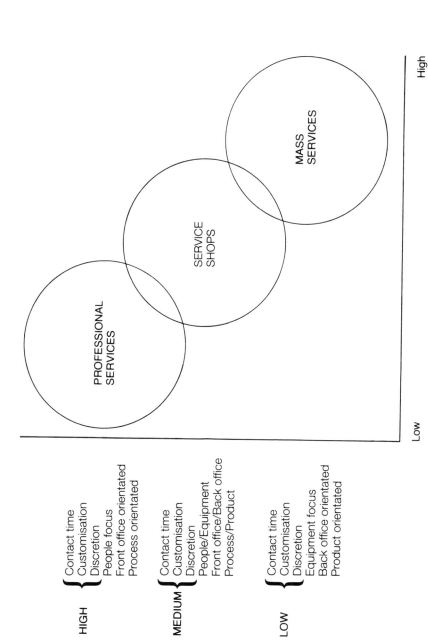

HIGH {
Contact time
Customisation
Discretion
People focus
Front office orientated
Process orientated

MEDIUM {
Contact time
Customisation
Discretion
People/Equipment
Front office/Back office
Process/Product

LOW {
Contact time
Customisation
Discretion
Equipment focus
Back office orientated
Product orientated

PROFESSIONAL SERVICES

SERVICE SHOPS

MASS SERVICES

Low

High

Number of customers processed by a typical unit per day

of the service innovation itself can be measured in terms of the other five dimensions (the service's competitiveness, profitability, productivity, quality, and flexibility).

In Tables 7.1 and 7.2 we identify a number of key issues for performance measurement across the six dimensions and give examples of measures of each dimension for the professional and mass service archetypes. These tables are meant to provide quick summaries of the book's findings to help managers recognise the control issues which will have to be addressed if they are to develop and improve their performance measurement systems. Greater detail on the measurement of each dimension and on the measurement systems of service shops may be obtained by consulting the appropriate chapter.

All companies, no matter what strategy or degree of competition they face and regardless of service type, will need to combine *feedforward control* via plans, standards, budgets and targets with *feedback control* via investigation of significant variances and the use of a balanced range of performance measures.

This approach to designing a balanced range of performance measures will not of itself guarantee sustainable competitive success, but research shows that this is what some successful service companies do.

7.3 How to motivate and reward employees

It is a key management task to get all employees to work together in the pursuit of strategic objectives. Participation and shared responsibility are central to this. An organisation's management information system and any incentive scheme linked to it are important in this context in several ways.

First, many things may be important to competitive success and should be measured, but they need not be part of any reward system. As a result, reward schemes may focus on a *sub-set* of the performance measures in the management information system.

Second, whilst much of the information system may be intended to *motivate and reward* managers for those things for which they are responsible and which they can control, it may also be perceived as threatening. Because the information system may be used to threaten or reward, managers may be tempted to manipulate it. There is therefore a risk that any information system which is also being used to evaluate and reward managers may cause them to take actions which are strategically

Table 7.1: Performance measurement in professional services

KEY ISSUES	PERFORMANCE DIMENSION	EXAMPLES OF MEASURES
Ability to win new customers Customer loyalty	COMPETITIVENESS	% success in tendering % repeat business Market share relative to key competitors
Control of staff costs Tracing of labour hours to individual jobs to aid pricing decisions	FINANCIAL PERFORMANCE	Staff costs Debtor and creditor days Value of work in progress Profit per service
Relationship building between customer and individual staff Negotiation of project specification with customer Measurement of customer satisfaction: use of unstructured, informal methods	QUALITY	Investment in training % non-chargeable: chargeable hours Adherence to project specification and delivery promise Customer satisfaction with various aspects of service
Management of short-term volume, specification and delivery speed flexibility Provision of flexibility through job scheduling, multiskilling, job rotation and staff discretion in dealing with customers	FLEXIBILITY	% orders lost due to late delivery Staff skill mix % hours bought in from other offices Customer satisfaction with delivery speed
Control of front office staff time	RESOURCE UTILISATION	Ratio of hours chargeable to client and non-chargeable hours Ratio of supervisors to staff
Measurement of the success of the innovation process and the innovation itself	INNOVATION	Number of new services New service introduction lead times % training spend invested in new services

Table 7.2: Performance measurement in mass services

KEY ISSUES	PERFORMANCE DIMENSION	EXAMPLES OF MEASURES
Ability to win new customers Customer loyalty	COMPETITIVENESS	No. of customers Market share Comparison of competitor prices and product ranges
Asset Turnover Control of labour and capital costs Costs difficult to trace to services due to high degree of cost allocation Profit per service difficult to measure	FINANCIAL PERFORMANCE	Return on net assets Working capital Profit per market segment
Relationship between customer and organisation Setting of clear customer expectations Measurement of customer satisfaction: use of formal, structured, sample-based methods	QUALITY	Equipment availability Product range Customer processing time Customer satisfaction with various aspects of service
Building volume, delivery speed and specification flexibility into the service design in the long term Use of level capacity strategies Employment of part-time and floating staff Use of price and promotion strategies to smooth demand	FLEXIBILITY	Monitoring of queue length No. of part time and floating staff Customer satisfaction with service availability
Utilisation of facilities, equipment and staff	RESOURCE UTILISATION	Costs per customer Revenue per customer Occupation ratios (e.g. % hotel rooms occupied)
Measurement of the success of the innovation process and the innovation itself	INNOVATION	% new: existing products and services R & D costs

undesirable. This may also cause misleading information to be fed into the information system, so causing top managers to make mistakes.

There is no easy way to avoid these problems. Participation in the design and running of such systems is no simple solution, for whilst it may lead to their acceptance and to behaviour congruent with organisational goals, it may also lead to playing the system and the building-in of unsuitable performance measures and targets. Individuals will differ in this respect, perhaps unpredictably.

The safest way of proceeding therefore is to tie performance-related rewards, for example bonuses, to the attainment of key success factors by *groups* of managers within an SBU *and* across the whole organisation (to give a rationale for co-operative interrelationships). In other words, rewards accrue to individuals but should be earned by group success. Finally, the key success factors that will determine the bonuses should be linked to *determinants* of competitive success, such as service quality, as well as to *results* such as profitability. Exhibit 7.1 shows an example of the successful use of a senior management bonus system.

Exhibit 7.1 BAA plc

Since privatisation as a near-monopoly the pressure on BAA to demonstrate publicly that financial performance is being maintained without detriment to service quality has, if anything, increased. BAA's control and performance measurement systems are therefore designed to give both financial and non-financial information at all organisational levels, with particular stress on four strategically key areas: *provision and utilisation of capacity, generation of income, utilisation of manpower* and *standards of service* provided to airport users. The management bonus scheme is linked to both financial performance and service levels. (Financial performance will, at least to some degree, subsume the first three key factors. Thus whilst manpower utilisation, for example, is strategically important and is therefore measured, it is not a formal part of the bonus system.) For each airport, the bonus is calculated on the basis of performance against a profit target, but even if this target is met it is possible for no bonus to be paid. The reason for this is that targets are also set for five key measures of customer satisfaction, and 20 per cent of the bonus is cut for every such target unmet.

This is an interesting and effective combination of a measure of results and five measures of determinants of competitive success being used in the design and operation of a bonus system.

7.4 *Towards the development of an integrated performance measurement system*

This book advocates measuring performance across six dimensions. In many of the service organisations that we studied data did exist across those six dimensions but was often not *integrated* into a system to support the monitoring and development of business strategy.

There are two key issues arising from this lack of integration. Firstly, it encourages the well documented *focusing on results*, competitiveness and financial measures, without measuring what is causing the success or otherwise of the organisation, that is the determinants: quality, flexibility, resource utilisation and innovation. Secondly, if data is not shared and discussed *trade-offs* between dimensions may be hidden (see previous chapters for discussions on trade-offs between dimensions).

We believe an integrated system of performance measures should be available to the whole management team, encouraging debate across *all* performance dimensions while recognising the interdependence of functional areas. In one of our case organisations these ideas were being reinforced by calling upon the marketing manager to present the financial results at board meetings (and vice-versa)!

Having established the need for a management information system that belongs to the whole management *team*, the question is who will facilitate the development of such a system?.

Management accountants have long fulfilled the role of collectors, collators, evaluators and distributors of management accounting information. The data set we are suggesting is wider than traditional management accounting reports, incorporating both financial and non-financial, quantitative and qualitative data. Some of the necessary information will fall outside the accountants' data collection methods and systems. For example, many competitiveness measures such as market share and market growth rate may be collected, monitored and interpreted by the marketing department. Some resource utilisation measures will be supplied by accountants, others such as human resource utilisation and equipment utilisation measures may be the province of personnel and operational managers.

Thus the accountants may usefully remain the chief collators and circulators of management information, but much of it may be collected, monitored and evaluated by its principal users.

The successful introduction of a new, improved management information system requires the involvement of *all* the management team; the accountants may be its principal custodians, but they should not have exclusive rights of access to and ownership over it. An opportunity exists for management accountants to play a growing role in integrating and co-ordinating the financial and non-financial data emanating from service activities, an opportunity which they should not ignore.

7.5 Conclusion

This book is about learning how to develop a management information system which will provide a balanced range of performance measures at strategic business unit level. The contention is that the selection of appropriate and relevant measures will depend on the type of service organisation in question, the environment in which it is competing and its chosen strategy. Our ideas reflect the findings of our research and the state-of-the-art at the time of writing. As the world of business does not stand still, continuing action is needed to generate new ideas about how to gain and retain a competitive advantage and adapt control and performance measurement systems accordingly.

7.6 Key points

- The design of a balanced range of performance measures should be done in three steps related to a company's competitive environment, chosen strategy and service type.

- Services operating in a turbulent competitive environment may need an interactive management information system to aid the learning process.

- Differentiators will need a range of performance measures slanted towards the feature(s) on which they are competing. Even pure 'cost leaders' will need to do more than just measure their resource utilisation and control costs.

- All companies will need to combine feedforward and feedback controls.

- Performance-related rewards should be made on the basis of group performance and should cover measures of determinants as well as results of competitive success.

- The successful introduction of a new management information system requires the involvement of all the management team. While the accountants may be its principal custodians all managers should have access to it.

References

1   Porter M., *Competitive Strategy*, Free Press, 1980 and *Competitive Advantage*, Free Press, 1985

2   Hill T.,. *Manufacturing Strategy – The Strategic Management of the Manufacturing Function*, Macmillan, 1985.